Angel Foods

Healthy Recipes for Heavenly Bodies

Cherie Soria

Cherie Soria (signature)

HEARTSTAR
PRODUCTIONS

Library of Congress Cataloging-in-Publication Data:
ISBN 0-9660329-0-X

To The Reader: This book is designed to offer information utilizing a natural way of eating. The information presented here shall not be interpreted or represent a claim for cure, diagnosis, treatment, or prevention of any disease. The concepts in this book have been practiced by thousands of people throughout the world as an alternative way of living and eating. The author and publisher assume no responsibility for improper application or interpretation of the natural laws contained herein. The author believes that each of us have the inherent right and primary obligation to develop to the fullest degree their physical, emotional, mental, and spiritual potential and offers this guide as assistance.

Printed in the United States of America.

Dedication & Acknowledgments

I dedicate this book to my teacher, Dr. Ann Wigmore, who influenced so many with her "Living Foods" diet. She speaks to me still.

Thanks to my number one fan and life partner, Neil Laurence, for his love and support in everything I do. Thanks also to all my students over the years who have tested my recipes and encouraged me to share the gift of food preparation. To Daniel Maziarts and Solara, who are responsible for my learning to commune with angels, much gratitude to you. Much appreciation to Shary Singer, who held my hand and patiently helped me unscramble my recipe files as we typeset this book. I want to express my gratitude to Morning Hullinger and everyone at Black Bear Press and to Chuck at Mendocino Graphics for their "can do" attitudes and loving support. Thanks to Kathryn Agrell of the Agrell Group and Jan Voltz for their editing assistance, and to Sid Freeman for her exquisite calligraphy. Lastly, a special thanks to all my guides and angels for leading me to Kim Waters, who created the incredibly sensitive and beautiful art that graces these pages.

Table of Contents

Introduction

"To love for the sake of being loved is human,
but to love for the sake of loving is angelic."
Alphonse de Lanartine

*A*ngel Foods is a Divinely inspired, unique guide to preparing delicious, nutritious foods from the plant kingdom. From appetizers to desserts, from sprouting to creating your own homemade nut and seed cheeses, this heavenly recipe book brings you a cornucopia of exciting and adventuresome foods. It includes a wide variety of cooked and uncooked lowfat recipes with an international flavor, tempting bits of food for thought, and even a how-to section on kitchen gardening. You'll find *Angel Foods* is also an illuminating cookbook filled with original angelic art and prayers of communion, encouraging you to honor the sacredness of food by bringing love and mindfulness to the act of food preparation.

Food, like all matter, is vibrational energy. When we consume it, the vibration of the food is transferred to us as vital life force. Therefore, the more fresh and alive the food is, the more life force we receive. Most of us can't see this life force with our naked eye, but it can be measured by Kirlian photography. This remarkable form of electrophotography captures the energy field around living things, and it's been proven in double blind studies that awareness of this life force strengthens and magnifies the subtle energy even more. When volunteers in scientific experiments directed their healing energy into water and the water was then given to plants, the plants responded by growing faster, larger, and more resistant to disease! We can do the same thing with our foods by focusing love energy into them as we prepare our meals.

We seldom think about honoring the foods we prepare or about being grateful for the nourishment they provide. What we want are foods that taste good and don't take too long to prepare or eat. We're advised that what we put into our bodies has a direct influence on our health and that we can benefit by eating more fresh plant-based foods. So, what we really need are light, health promoting, simple, delicious meals that are prepared with love and caring—not only because they'll be served to those we love (including ourselves), but also out of respect and gratitude for the food itself.

I have always loved preparing foods, but it wasn't until recently that I consciously began to bring my connection with nature and the Divine into the kitchen with me. Like many people, I was opening up to a new spiritual consciousness affecting all aspects of my life. It was a natural progression for my newfound awareness to follow me into my favorite art form—preparing delicious, nutritious meals. Now, as I wash and prepare each individual fruit or vegetable, my eyes feast on its' beauty. I appreciate its' uniqueness and feel grateful and honored to be the one combining it with other foods to create tasty, nourishing cuisine for myself and my loved ones. I also use this time as a meditation and an opportunity to commune with my celestial guardians and other Divine energies of love. I have discovered that creating healthy meals can be a spiritual experience and when our bodies are sound and strong, it's easy for our spirits to soar!

Just imagine... every time you open the refrigerator or dip into the fruit bowl or harvest your sprouts you feel immensely grateful for these edible blessings. When preparing a meal, you infuse the foods you've chosen with Divine love and simultaneously feel the outpouring of love from each ingredient as you handle it. You feel a profound sense of appreciation and gratitude for the foods. When you do this, you may begin to experience a spiritual connection to the food; a feeling of being blessed by simply being in the moment. Even the most menial tasks can become sacred acts when one's conscious awareness is tuned to love.

If merging with the vibrational essence of food and talking to angels and other higher forces sounds a little over the top to you, all I can say is—give it a try. When your mind wanders away from the food, have a "talk with spirit" or recite "angelic communions" and "intentions". Many examples of these are included throughout this book to assist you in creating your own communications with spirit. When you're connected to your "higher self" and you prepare food in this way, using the freshest, most beautiful ingredients available (preferably organically grown), it's natural to honor and protect the inherent perfection of the food by cooking and processing it as little as possible.

Today, even doctors and scientists are emphasizing the importance of raw and living foods in our diet due to the depletion of essential vitamins, enzymes, friendly bacteria, and other important microorganisms caused by unnecessary cooking. Modern scientific medicine is finally catching up with traditional wisdom and helping us prevent the diseases caused by the Standard American Diet (appropriately know as SAD)!

I do not mean to imply that one can never again eat cooked foods—I still enjoy cooking and going out to eat. This book was not intended for only "raw food purists". In fact, nearly half the recipes in this book require some cooking. *Angel Foods* offers a balanced approach to healthful eating in suggesting that consuming more uncooked and living foods could benefit us all. Of course most people aren't accustomed to eating a lot of raw foods, so I recommend easing into it. This can be done by adding one uncooked dish to your daily intake and increasing it as you feel ready. For many people the summer months are the easiest time to embrace raw foods, however, raw doesn't necessarily mean cold. Foods may be warmed to well above body temperature and still maintain their life force. A good rule of thumb is; if you stick your finger in it, it should feel warm—not hot.

The most important thing I wish to express in *Angel Foods* is that you commune with your food when you buy or grow it, wash it, peel it, slice it, and of course, when you eat it! Even if you stop on the way home from work and pick up a pizza, be grateful for its' blessings. It's not necessary to deprive yourself of what you want; but you'll find more and more that what you want is also what's in your best interest. So if you eat that pizza, tell your celestial guardians you have a special treat for them—pizza! If it's not something you do all the time, and you infuse it with love and eat it mindfully, chances are it will do no harm.

Angel Foods promises to leave you with far more than 240 great recipes. It offers a new way of relating to the time spent preparing food. Remember, if you prepare food when you hate the thought of going in the kitchen, you could transfer that energy into the food! Instead, consider eating simple raw foods for dinner—they take little preparation, almost no cleanup, and leave you feeling light. First and foremost infuse the food you eat with love. Intend that the time spent around food to be loving, peaceful time. You'll be renewed and infused with love energy, and those you share your delicious meals with will feel it too!

Chapter One

Earth Angel Answers

A Talk with Spirit about Oneness

Spirit, flow into my heart, bringing love and light so that I may see I am one with all things. Help me let go of judgment, break through the walls of separation and know that all the earthly inhabitants and I are one. We are all spirit, love, energy, and vibration. We are sparks of Divine Light from our Creator, the Source of All That Is. Please help me by increasing my awareness of the light in everyone and everything. Help me become more mindful by guiding me to live in the moment, by teaching me to recognize the sacredness of everything I do, and by helping me to perceive the subtler energies and vibrations that connect us all.

Please assist me in creating an aura of sacredness around the act of food preparation. When I prepare food, help me be focused with love and appreciation for its presence. Allow Universal Life Force to flow through me and infuse that gift of nourishment with additional love and light. Help me perceive the food's energy increase as it responds to the pure love of the One Divine Source. I love you, I bless you, I am one with you and All That Is.

Love is the Answer to Every Question!

As we evolve and learn, our truths often change. Health "truths," like all scientific knowledge, are subject to reinterpretation as new knowledge comes to light or old knowledge is rediscovered. New research is constantly replacing yesterday's facts about what's best for our bodies and which foods may be deemed healthiest. Every day, it seems, new information is released that challenges our ideas about fats, sugars, carbohydrates, proteins, vitamins, minerals, enzymes, and the role they play when it comes to our health. After twenty-five years as a "food scientist" and as an international instructor in the art of vegan and vegetarian food preparation, I have come to realize and appreciate that just as people differ in their personalities, so does each body differ in its response to food, as well as to thoughts and emotions; and that all these elements combined with exercise and lifestyle work together to create our health. In the following, I have endeavored to answer, to the best of my experience and knowledge, the most often-asked questions that I have received in my classes.

We hear a lot about enzymes. How can we know we're getting enough?

Enzymes are a necessary component in the digestion of foods. When foods are heated above 115 to 120 degrees F., enzymatic action ceases, as does the life force of the food. If your diet consists of more cooked foods than raw foods and you're concerned about getting enough enzymes, eat more uncooked foods, drink raw vegetable juices and/or take enzyme supplements.

Do our bodies produce enzymes?

According to research, our bodies produce enzymes, but not for the purpose of digestion. We manufacture a limited supply of enzymes for all our vital systems to function. A lack of enzymes causes aging and age-related illnesses. When we eat cooked foods lacking in enzymes, we deplete our resources in order to use them for digestion. A high enzyme content is one reason why raw foods are reputed to promote such good health and longevity.

Adding more raw foods to my diet seems like a lot of work. How can I get started?

Many people find it easy to begin by eating raw fruit in the morning, as a light breakfast or 1/2 hour before their regular breakfast. By adding a raw salad or other raw foods to the afternoon or evening meal, they experience even more energy and vitality. Eating food in its natural state (uncooked) increases awareness of the perfection of nature. Once people make this change, the foods they are most attracted to are the ones that make them feel the best. After awhile, the desire for foods lacking in life force diminishes.

What about winter? Don't we need hot foods when it's cold outside?

Chilled foods can be cooling in a winter climate. I suggest gently warming foods so they are warmer than body temperature. Also, take fruits and vegetables out of the refrigerator early or put them in warm water before preparing them. Another idea is to start with a cup of warm soup before your meal, so that a raw salad or other uncooked food won't chill your body.

How can I change my family's eating habits?

We can't change others; we can only be examples. Even children need to exercise free will. Discover what healthful foods your family likes and create meals around those. Then add one new food at a time. Don't give up if they don't like it the first time; prepare it differently next time. Kids who don't like a vegetable cooked will often like it raw with a dip, especially if it's cut into fun shapes! Children also love growing sprouts and young greens. They enjoy being included in food preparation. Even very young children can help with salads and other uncooked foods. Stories about the foods, their origin, how they grow, and how grateful we are to have them, are all helpful in sparking children's interest in eating healthful foods. Include your children in your communions with the food and tell them about their Guardian Angels. Use this special time together to bring a spiritual awareness into their lives.

How important is it to grow my own sprouts and greens?

Sprouting takes only minutes a day. Once you've tuned in to the life force present in foods, you'll find great joy in growing your own. As you nurture them, you are nurtured. When you eat them you can taste and feel their vitality. You are, essentially, eating the love you give! Sprouts and even young greens can be purchased at many health food stores, and though they are more expensive than those lovingly produced at home, we're happy for their availability. Sprouts and young greens are teeming with life force! They are, after all, still living!

We hear a lot about oils. Which are best?

Choosing the healthiest oil is one of those ever-changing truths. When I cook with oil, I choose olive oil. It's best to use as little oil as possible and avoid frying at high temperatures. For salads, a small amount of flax oil is recommended for it's Omega 3 benefits. I suggest no more than 2 to 3 teaspoons per day due to its estrogen-producing qualities. A few drops of toasted sesame oil adds a nice Oriental flavor; corn oil works well in baking; and peanut oil is my first choice for high-heat wok cooking. It's a good idea to limit the use of oils due to the free radicals they create. Always keep oils refrigerated so they don't become rancid, again creating those rascally free radicals. Whole food fats such as avocados and soaked or cultured nuts and seeds are always preferable to oils separated from their foods. As your tastes change, and they naturally do when you begin eating more natural, uncooked foods, you'll find that oily foods will appeal to you less.

Why is it important to soak nuts and seeds?

Soaking nuts and seeds removes the growth inhibitors that impair digestion. This allows them to germinate, so they contain more life force. During the germination process, each begins the transition from nut or seed to vegetable. Going a step further and allowing them to ferment makes them even more digestible and infuses them with precious lactobacillus bifidus and acidophilus. Check out Chapter two, *Gardening Angels are Sprouting Up Everywhere*, for more on sprouting and germinating, and Chapter three, *Angels Have Culture,* for more on fermented foods such as nut and seed cheeses.

What are the benefits of fermented foods?

Cultured, or fermented foods, like nut cheeses and yogurts, vege-krauts, unpasteurized miso, and *Rejuvilac* are easily digested foods containing various lactobacillus bacteria. These friendly flora are important aids in the health of our intestinal tracts, promoting a healthy environment for nutrient production and assimilation. They are also rich in enzymes and B vitamins. Nut and seed cheeses can be seasoned with herbs or sweetened. See Chapter five, *Angelic Appetizers & Sinful Spreads,* for some delicious recipes!

What are the best types of sweeteners to use?

Fruit sweeteners and fruit syrups are best in fruit dishes. Brown rice syrup, Sucanat® (dehydrated cane sweetener), and pure maple syrup work well with grains and other starches and nut and seed cheeses. I avoid the use of honey, since it's an animal product.

What do you consider the most important thing to remember for those of us just venturing into this way of eating?

Realize that you don't need to make big sacrifices to eat a healthy diet. This does not need to be achieved overnight, so ease into it. Eat the foods you enjoy most. If you like something cooked, chances are, you may enjoy it as much uncooked! Remember that what you eat is important, but what *you think* about what you eat is equally important. So whatever you eat, bless it, enjoy it, and know that it is fulfilling your highest interest. If you can't believe that, perhaps you don't want it after all!

Who are the Kitchen Gadget Devas?

No matter how much you enjoy cooking, it helps to have a little help from your friends, the kitchen gadgets devas, who want nothing more than to make your life easier!

Blender—a must for any kitchen; it blends, purees, and mixes sauces, dressings, and smoothies.

Citrus Juicer—available in manual or electric; it's a handy gadget for making citrus juice.

Colander—a perforated bowl, necessary for straining pasta, washing greens, and making nut cheese.

Fruit and Vegetable Juice Extractor—an electronic juicer essential to a healthful kitchen. It's not recommended for citrus unless it has a special citrus attachment. Some juicers also make "ice creams" from fresh frozen fruit, homogenized baby foods, nut butters, and other delights!

Food Processor—the most versatile kitchen appliance; it does everything a blender does, as well as mincing, grinding, chopping, slicing, and shredding. Great for making sauerkraut, Essene breads, zucchini pasta, and other foods presented in this book.

Food Dehydrator—removes moisture from foods and warms them using low temperatures while retaining 75% of the enzymes present in the food. Great for making fruit leathers, seasoned sprouted nuts and seeds, and for "cooking" foods without destroying their entire enzyme content.

Garlic Press—a handy item that eliminates peeling, mincing, and mashing garlic.

Hand Blender/Beater—a small, electric, hand-held appliance that's great for making salad dressings and sauces. It's inserted into a small bowl, a glass, or a saucepan to emulsify liquids.

Knife Sharpener—available in many styles; it is essential in any kitchen.

Knives—every kitchen needs at least a paring knife, a 5-inch serrated knife, a chef's knife, and a sharpening steel.

Lime Squeezer—a handy gadget if you use a lot of lime juice; it resembles a large garlic press.

Non-stick Pans—come in many sizes and are important for cooking without the use of oil.

Nut Grinder or Seed Mill—pulverizes nuts, seeds, spices, and sugars.

Salad Spinner—is used for washing and drying greens.

Slicer/dicer/shredder—a manual device that enables the user to slice, dice, or shred perfectly.

Springform Pan—used for making cakes; the sides are removable for ease of serving.

Sprouting Bags—a mesh bag with a drawstring, used for sprouting and making nut and seed cheese.

Sushi Mat—a 9 x 10-inch, bamboo mat used exclusively to assist in rolling *Japanese Sushimaki*.

Wheatgrass Juicer—available in manual or electric, it's only used for making wheatgrass juice.

What in Heaven's Name is Agar-Agar?

Agar-agar is a colorless sea vegetable that is used to replace gelatine in cooking, because gelatine is rendered from animal tissues. There are many healthful, if unusual, products recommended in this book, most of which are available through health food stores and supermarkets. Buy one or two each week, and familiarize yourself with them; in no time, they will cease to be unusual.

Arrowroot—a healthful replacement for cornstarch.
Basmati Rice—a wonderfully aromatic East Indian rice; it takes only 30 minutes to cook.
Braggs Liquid Aminos®—a salty, liquid seasoning made from vegetable protein.
Brown Rice Syrup—a sweet, thick syrup used to replace honey (which is an animal product).
Buckwheat Groats—whole, husked, buckwheat; it is sprouted, and used in cereals, and breads.
Carob—naturally sweet, and nutritious; it is often used as a chocolate substitute.
Cultured or Fermented Foods—contain fresh lactobacillus bacteria; is an important digestive aid.
Gluten Flour—wheat flour with the starch removed; it can be used as a binder in loaves and patties,
    used to make seitan, or added to bread recipes to increase protein and improve overall results.
Kamut—a nonhybridized ancient wheat, easier to digest than common wheat.
Millet—a yellow, aromatic grain; it is cooked like rice, or sprouted and added to cereals and breads.
Miso— salty, fermented, soy or grain and/or soy product used in soups, sauces, gravies, and spreads.
Nutritional Yeast—is high in minerals and B vitamins; it has a delicious, mild cheese flavor.
Pure Maple Syrup—100% maple syrup extracted from maple trees, with no sugar added.
Rejuvilac—a fermented grain beverage containing acidophilus; used as a digestive aid (see pg. 15).
Sea Vegetables—flavorful, ocean grown vegetables; they are high in vitamins and minerals.
Seitan—a meat-like vegetable protein made from gluten flour (see above).
Sprouts—germinated nuts, seeds, beans, or legumes; can be eaten raw or cooked (see pg. 7).
Sucanat®—dehydrated sugar cane juice; it is a whole food sweetener.
Sunflower Greens—young, green sunflower plants; they can be grown indoors (see pg. 11).
Tahini—sesame seed butter; it is added to gravies, dressings, and sauces; and is high is calcium.
Tamari—a wheat-free, traditionally brewed soy sauce; it has a very salty flavor.
Tempeh—a high protein, cultured soybean product; it can replace meat in most recipes.
Tofu—a soft, delicately flavored, soybean curd; it can be used in an infinite variety of recipes.
Vegan Egg Replacer—made from tapioca flour; it can replace eggs in most recipes.
Wheatgrass—young grass grown from wheat; it's juice is high in chlorophyll (see pg. 11).

Chapter Two

Gardening Angels are Sprouting Up Everywhere

A Talk with Spirit about Conscious Awareness

Divine Presence, fill me with conscious awareness of All That Is. Help me to see my own light and experience that part of me that is pure spirit. Assist me in knowing that I always was and always will be energy, light and love, and that I am pure consciousness expressing myself in human form. Increase my awareness of the subtle energies, so that I may recognize the connectedness in all things and release the veil of separation.

I open my heart and allow love and light to flow in from the Divine Source of All That Is. I ask to experience a new awareness of the consciousness in all things, so that I may fully appreciate the blessings present in this food and in my life. As I focus love and gratitude upon these gifts, I feel their life force increase and I am filled with Divine Light. I love you, I bless you, I am one with you and All That Is.

Gardening Angels are Sprouting up Everywhere!

Kitchen gardening is fun and easy and requires very little time to reap the rewards. Germinating seeds takes as little as six hours of soaking. Growing young sunflower greens requires only ten days from soaking to harvest. No weeding is required and there are no pests or predators to contend with. As far as space is concerned, sprouts, wheatgrass, and sunflower greens can even be grown in a hotel room or while traveling in a motor home. I know because I've done it!

There's no fancy, expensive equipment needed to grow greens or sprouts, and for those who require the freedom to travel, kitchen gardening is the ticket! When you need to leave town unexpectedly, you can either take your sprouts with you or put them in the refrigerator for a few days and they'll be fine. When you return, simply take them out, rinse, and they will resume growing. Flats of greens can also be refrigerated if you have the space, or put in a cool place out of direct light to slow their growth. Or, you can harvest them and store them in the refrigerator.

Children love to grow sprouts and young greens. They can almost see changes from one hour to the next! They enjoy rinsing and pampering "the babies" and helping them thrive. Sprouts make great finger foods for children, and they can be added to salads, soups and sandwiches. Getting kids involved in kitchen gardening is one of the most valuable gifts you can give them!

Sprouts and young greens are "living foods" containing concentrated life force. They provide nutrients and vibrational essences unsurpassed by other produce. The process of soaking allows germination to take place. When a nut or seed germinates, it begins the journey from dormant seed to young vegetable. During this transformation, it awakens in a burst of energy, predigesting its proteins which makes it easier for us to digest and assimilate. Sprouts and young plants contain more energy during this short period of their lives than at any other time in their maturity, so they are more nutrient dense, enzyme rich, and life generating. They promote cellular renewal and therefore are rejuvenating and revitalizing to our bodies. Sprouts are literally fountains of youth, increasing our energy and vitality as we merge their essence with our own.

Sound interesting? Read on and see how simple kitchen gardening can be!

The Joys of Sprouting
Nuts, Seeds, Grains, and Legumes

Germinating nuts, and sprouting seeds, grains, and legumes is easy! All you need are a few jars, plastic screen from the hardware store, and rubber bands. Choose jars that are 1 quart to 1 gallon in size, depending upon whether you are sprouting full term or simply soaking to allow germination. Measure the mouth of the jar, allowing a couple of inches to drape over the sides, and cut the screen with ordinary scissors. Add your seeds and fill the jar with water. Cover the jar with screen and secure with a rubber band. After soaking, allow them to drain thoroughly in a dish rack; then put the jars in a dark place for 8 to 12 hours. Rinse until the water is clear and drain again. To develop chlorophyll in seeds such as alfalfa, place them in the light for 2 to 3 days prior to harvest, continuing to rinse every 8 to 12 hours.

Nuts:

To make cheese, nuts require soaking only. However if you're using them for snacking, allow 24 hours additional germination time. They keep in the refrigerator for a week and are ready to be added to blended drinks or to eat as a snack. Choose a jar that will allow the nuts to nearly double in volume.

Hard Nuts: Almonds, Brazil Nuts, Filberts & Macadamias—Soak 24 hours, rinse and drain
Soft Nuts: Cashews, Pecans, & Walnuts—Soak for 12 hours, rinse and drain

Seeds:

Seeds such as sunflower, sesame, and pumpkin also need only soaking in order to make cheese. Otherwise, allow another 12 to 24 hours germination time. Choose jars that will allow the seeds to double in volume. Sprouts that require the development of chlorophyll, such as alfalfa, clover, radish, chive, onion, and garlic, need lots of room to grow. So give them a big jar (1/4 cup of alfalfa seeds will yield a gallon of sprouts) and, 2 to 3 days prior to harvesting, give them plenty of bright light. When alfalfa and clover sprouts are ready, rinse them in a large bowl of water to remove hulls.

Alfalfa, Radish, and **Clover Seeds**—Soak 8 hours, rinse and drain twice daily for 6 days
Chive, Onion, and **Garlic Seeds**—Soak 8 hours, rinse and drain three times daily for 10 days
Flax, Sesame, **Sunflower,** and **Pumpkin**—Soak 6 hours, rinse and drain twice daily for 1 to 2 days

Grains:

Grains require soaking, plus at least 24 hours sprouting time, rinsing thoroughly at 8- to 12-hour intervals. They'll keep in the refrigerator for more than a week, ready to be added to blended drinks, cereals, breads, or to be eaten as a snack. Choose jars that will allow the grains to double in volume. For traveling, fine mesh sprouting bags also may be used; however, more rinsing is required.

Buckwheat Groats—Soak for 8 hours, rinse thoroughly, and drain twice daily for 1 to 2 days
Kamut, Hard Wheat and Soft Wheat—Soak 8 hours, rinse and drain twice daily for 1 to 2 days
Rye and Triticale—Soak for 8 hours, rinse and drain twice daily for 1 to 2 days

Beans and Legumes:

Beans and legumes require soaking plus at least 24 hours sprouting time, rinsing thoroughly at 8- to 12-hour intervals. They'll keep in the refrigerator for a week or more, ready to be added to blended soups, salads, main dishes, or to be eaten as a snack. Choose jars that will allow them to triple in volume. For traveling, sprouting bags are handy; however, more rinsing will be required.

Lentils and Whole (dried) Peas—Soak 12 hours, rinse and drain twice daily for 2 days
Adzuki and Mung Beans—Soak 12 hours, rinse and drain twice daily for 2 to 3 days
Black-Eyed Peas and Garbanzos—Soak 12 hours, rinse and drain 3 times daily for 3 to 4 days

Basic Sprouting Chart

Variety	Dry Measure	Soak	Rinse	Harvest	Yield
Soft nuts	1/2 cup	12 hours	a.m. & p.m.	1–2 days	3/4 cup
Hard nuts	1/2 cup	24 hours	a.m. & p.m.	1–2 days	3/4 cup
Alfalfa seeds, etc.*	1/4 cup	8 hours	a.m. & p.m.	6–10 days	1 gallon
Sunflower seeds, etc.*	1/4 cup	6–8 hours	a.m. & p.m.	1–2 days	1/2–1 cup
Grains	1/4 cup	8 hours	a.m. & p.m.	2–3 days	1/2–1 cup
Beans & Legumes	1/4 cup	12 hours	a.m. & p.m.	2–3 days	1/2–1cup

Note: Always rinse sprouts until the water is clear, and drain thoroughly in a dish rack.
*See *Seeds* opposite page.

The Joys of Kitchen Gardening

Growing your own greens can be a wonderfully spiritual experience that allows you to tune into nature in a very special way: nurturing it and being nurtured by it. You can watch your greens respond to your tender loving care, and feel the strength of their life-force when you care for, harvest, and ingest them. Unlike other forms of gardening, there is no great space requirement, no weeds to pull, no pests or predators to worry about, and it takes only a week to ten days to harvest your crop!

Growing wheat grass for juicing, and young greens, like sunflower and buckwheat lettuce, for salads, is easy and economical. Wheat grass juice is a high-chlorophyll drink that helps to cleanse the blood and build it through oxygenation. Sunflower and buckwheat greens are great in salads and other dishes that call for leafy greens. They also are an excellent source of vitamins and minerals and are rich in enzymes. Beyond the measurable nutrients that these high-energy foods contain, exist the vibrational essences. Each plant has its own frequency signature, which aids in the healing of different areas of our bodies. When the young plant is freshly cut and ingested immediately, its life force is peaking. When you care for a plant yourself, you can become tuned into this and *feel* the presence of the plant's energy. Kitchen gardening enables you to commune with nature and the Divine!

ALL YOU NEED to begin kitchen gardening is seeds, jars, plastic screen from the hardware store, rubber bands, good organic soil, and a few cafeteria trays or garden flats. You may use your own composted soil or purchase good organic soil by the bag. It takes only about 1 1/2 to 2 quarts of soil per 14" x 18" tray. (See *The Joys of Sprouting,* pg. 8, for how to sprout the seeds.) To determine how much seed to soak, see the chart below.

Indoor Gardening Chart

Variety	Measure *	Soak	Sprout	Harvest Ht.	Ready In	Yield
Wheat, Kamut	1 1/4 cups	8–12 hours	1 day	6–7 inches	6–8 days	8–10 ounces juice
Sunflower	1 1/2 cups	8–12 hours	1 day	6–7 inches	7–9 days	1 pound (approx.)
Buckwheat	1 cup	8–12 hours	1 day	6–7 inches	7–9 days	1 pound (approx.)

* Dry measure, per 14" x 18" cafeteria tray

How to Grow Wheatgrass:

For the best wheatgrass, buy organic, hard red winter wheat berries from your health food store. Once the wheat berries have been soaked and sprouted, as previously described, they're ready for planting. Spread 1 1/2 quarts of soil evenly in a cafeteria tray that is 3/4 of an inch deep. Distribute the sprouted wheat evenly over the soil, 1/2 inch from the edges. Moisten with 2 to 3 cups of water. Invert another cafeteria tray and place it on the top; then put it aside for a couple of days. When the grass has pushed up the tray, remove it. Place the grass in the light and water it daily. Harvest your grass, as you need it, using scissors or a serrated knife. Cut close to the soil, thanking it for its offering, and discard or compost the remaining root bed.

How to Grow Sunflower Greens:

Buy organic, raw sunflower seeds in the shell, which is available through health foods stores, or order them using the *Resource Guide* (see pg. 217). When they've been soaked and sprouted, as previously described, they're ready for planting. Spread 1 quart of soil evenly in a cafeteria tray, 1/2 inch deep. Distribute the sprouted seeds over the top, and lay another quart of soil evenly over the first. Water the soil with 2 to 3 cups of water, so it is wet but not flooded. Invert another cafeteria tray and place it on top; then put it aside for several days. When the growth of the young sunflowers begins to push up on the tray, remove it. Put the sunflowers under good light and water daily. Harvest your greens as you need them, or all at once, using scissors or a serrated knife. Cut stalks close to the soil, thanking them for their offering. Sunflowers will provide a second harvest from the slower growing seeds, so continue watering them until they all mature.

How to Grow Buckwheat Lettuce:

Purchase organic, buckwheat in the shell, which is available through health foods stores or can be ordered through the *Resource Guide* (see pg. 217). When the seeds have been soaked and sprouted, as previously described, they're ready for planting. Spread 1 1/2 quarts of soil evenly in a cafeteria tray, 3/4 of an inch deep. Distribute the sprouted buckwheat over the soil and moisten with 2 to 3 cups of water. Invert another cafeteria tray and place it on the top; then put it aside for several days. When the buckwheat begins to push up on the tray remove it. Place the buckwheat under good light and water daily. Harvest your greens as you need them, or all at once, using scissors or a serrated knife. Cut stalks close to the soil, thanking them for their offering. Continue watering for a second harvest.

Chapter Three

Angels Have Culture

A Talk with Spirit about Opening up to Change

Divine Energies of Love, please assist me in opening up and culturing a change in my thinking and in my life. Help me move forward without resistance, letting go of that which no longer serves my best interest. Help me feel safe with change, knowing that I have your Divine guidance. I desire to learn and experience new things that will add to my mental, physical, and spiritual well-being. I trust that you will be next to me, illuminating my path, as I walk into the unknown. I am grateful for your assistance in helping me to trust the process of life and expect the unexpected.

As I focus my love and gratitude upon these foods, I sense and feel their life force increase and I am filled with Light from the Divine Source of All That Is. I welcome our union and the nourishment that it provides. I love you, I bless you, I am one with you.

Recipes at a Glance

Cultured or fermented foods like nut and seed cheeses, non-dairy kefirs and yogurts, sauerkraut, and *Rejuvilac* are not only rich in enzymes and friendly flora, but are delicious additions to any diet.

*Guardian Angel,
I trust you to
assist me at all times
in everything I do.*

Salute! To your health!

Rejuvilac is a fermented grain beverage, which can also be helpful in culturing nut and seed cheeses. It costs just pennies to make and is one of the most health-promoting drinks on the planet. It's high in enzymes and contains important lactobacillus bifidus—both of which are necessary for good digestion and assimilation.

Rejuvilac is easy to make and is well worth the two minutes, morning and night, that it takes to rinse the sprouts. Other than grain, the only vital ingredient in this healthful beverage is purified water. (Chlorinated water will kill the precious bacteria you wish to cultivate and your beverage will smell rotten instead of cheese-like or whey-like.) Expect the odor and flavor to change from day to day—the first day being the strongest, with your second and third harvests becoming more tart and lemony. I suggest using second or third day *Rejuvilac* for making cheese, since it is milder in flavor.

So that you have fresh *Rejuvilac* every day, begin sprouting a new batch of grain every three days. (This will require two large jars covered with plastic mesh, and secured with rubber bands—see pg. 8, *The Joys of Sprouting*.) To make life easier, consider choosing two days a week, such as Wednesday and Saturday, to begin a new batch. This means stretching one batch to four harvests instead of three, but you will always know when to start your sprouts without having to calculate the days. Discard any left-over *Rejuvilac* after twenty-four hours of storage. To enhance the flavor, add one herbal fruit tea bag per quart and steep for two hours (Celestial Seasonings® makes wonderful fruit blends), or add a squeeze of lemon with a little sweetener and you have *Rejuvilac* lemon-aid!

Rejuvilac
(Fermented Grain Beverage)

makes 2 quarts each day for 3 days

1/4 cup soft wheat berries
1/4 cup whole rye
2 gallons purified or spring water (non-chlorinated)

6 Celestial Seasonings® Strawberry-Kiwi or Wild Cherry
    Blackberry tea bags (optional)

1. Day # 1: In the morning, combine the grains in a gallon jar, cover with plastic mesh, and secure with a rubber band. Add at least 2 quarts of water and soak for 8 to 12 hours.
2. That evening, pour off the soak water, rinse with tap water, and drain well. Place jar in a cool, dark place and allow to sprout.
3. Day #2: In the morning, rinse and drain again, and repeat this process in the evening.
4. Day #3: In the morning, rinse once with tap water and drain well. Rinse again with purified water, drain, and add 2 quarts of purified water. Put jar in a cool dark place and allow to ferment for 36 to 48 hours. (It will ferment sooner in hot weather.)
5. Day #5: In the morning, pour your first batch of fermented water (*Rejuvilac*) into a container and store in the refrigerator to drink that day. Pour 2 more quarts of purified water onto the sprouted grains (do not rinse!) and allow to ferment for another 24 hours.
6. Day #6: In the morning, repeat step #5.
7. Day #7: The final morning, pour your third batch into a container and store in the refrigerator to drink that day. (To stretch your harvest to a fourth day, repeat step #5.)
8. Discard grains and wash jar well with soap and water.

I recommend beginning with small quantities of *Rejuvilac* so that your body can become accustomed to its cleansing properties. Eight ounces a day working up to a quart a day is adequate for most people.

Guardian Angel,
please help me
be at peace
in mind and body.

Luscious milks and creams can be created easily from nuts and seeds. Almonds are hailed as the "queen of nuts" because of their alkaline nature, and therefore are more health promoting than other milks. They are delicious on cereals, sweetened and poured over fruit, or added to blender drinks and sherbets.

Guardian Angel,
please help me
live in harmony with
all of God's creatures.

Almond Milk

makes 1 quart

1 cup whole raw almonds, soaked in 3 cups water for 24 hours, drained and rinsed
3 cups purified or spring water (divided use)
1/2 Tbsp. Sucanat® (dehydrated sugar cane juice)
1/2 tsp. vanilla extract (optional)

1. Put almonds in a blender with 1 1/2 of cups water and purée until smooth and creamy. (Use as much or as little water as necessary to keep the blender mixing.)
2. Pour purée through a fine mesh strainer to remove almond skins and pulp. Put remaining water and pulp back into blender and purée again. Repeat, straining pulp from milk. After pressing out all milk, discard pulp.
3. Stir in sweetener and vanilla, and enjoy!

Almond Cream

makes 1 pint

1 cup whole raw almonds, soaked in 3 cups water for 24 hours, drained and rinsed
1 1/2 cups purified or spring water (non-chlorinated)
1/2 Tbsp. Sucanat® (dehydrated sugar cane juice)
1/2 tsp. vanilla extract (optional)

1. Put almonds in a blender with water and purée until smooth and creamy. (Use more water, if needed, to keep the blender mixing.)
2. Pour cream through a mesh strainer to remove almond skins and pulp. After pressing out all cream, discard pulp.
3. Stir in sweetener and vanilla, and enjoy!

Cashew Milk

makes 1 quart

1 cup raw cashews, soaked in 3 cups water for 12 hours
    and rinsed
3 cups purified or spring water
1 Tbsp. Sucanat® (dehydrated sugar cane juice)
    or pure maple syrup
1/2 tsp. vanilla

1. Put cashews in a blender with water and purée until smooth and creamy.
2. Stir in sweetener and vanilla, and enjoy! Will keep in refrigerator for up to one week.

Cashew Cream

makes 1 pint

1 cup raw cashews, soaked in 3 cups water for 12 hours
    and rinsed
1 1/2 cups purified or spring water
1 Tbsp. Sucanat® (dehydrated sugar cane juice)
    or pure maple syrup
1/2 tsp. vanilla

1. Put cashews in a blender with water and purée until smooth and creamy. (Add more water, if needed, to keep blender mixing.)
2. Stir in sweetener and vanilla, and enjoy! Will keep in refrigerator for up to one week.

This thick, creamy nut cream is a perfect substitute for dairy cream, and since the nut is soft, without skins or hulls, there is no straining required—it blends smoothly and completely. The thickness is only dependent upon the amount of water used, so it can be anything from a thick cream to a thin milk.

*Guardian Angel,
please help me
look for the
Angelic Presence
in all life.*

This is a delicious yogurt drink that will make your tummy smile. Culturing the almonds predigests the protein while creating friendly flora, making it very easy to digest. Make it at night and it'll be ready for you to enjoy in the morning! (For tips on how to peel almonds, see *Insights* below.)

*Guardian Angel,
please help me
see myself transformed
into Love and Light.*

Almond Kefir

makes 1 quart

2 cups whole raw almonds, soaked in 3 cups water for 24 hours, rinsed, and peeled (see *Insights* below)
3 cups purified water or *Rejuvilac* (see pg. 15)
2 Tbsp. Sucanat® (dehydrated sugar cane juice) or pure maple syrup
1 tsp. vanilla or 1/8 tsp. almond extract

1. Put almonds in a blender with enough water or *Rejuvilac* to cover, and purée until smooth and creamy. (Use as much or as little liquid as necessary for desired consistency.)
2. Pour into a glass jar and cover with a clean towel. Put it in a warm (not hot) place for 6 to 12 hours (depending upon temperature and desired tartness) and allow to ferment.
3. Stir in sweetener, add extract, and enjoy! Will keep in refrigerator for up to one week.

Note: Using *Rejuvilac* instead of water speeds up the fermentation time and creates a more tart flavor.

Insights: To remove skins from soaked almonds, place them in warm (not hot) water for an hour before peeling. Taking a small, unserrated paring knife in one hand, while holding an almond in the other, scrape one long edge of the almond to loosen the skin. The remainder of the skin will simply slide off!

Cashew Kefir

makes 1 quart

2 cups raw cashews, soaked in 3 cups water for 12 hours
and rinsed
3 cups *Rejuvilac* (see pg. 15)
2 Tbsp. Sucanat® (dehydrated sugar cane juice)
1 tsp. vanilla

1. Put cashews in a blender with enough *Rejuvilac* to cover, and
purée until smooth and creamy. (Use as much or as little
Rejuvilac as necessary for desired consistency.)
2. Pour into a glass jar and cover with a clean towel. Put it in a
warm (not hot) place for 6 to 12 hours (depending upon
temperature and desired tartness) and allow to ferment.
3. Stir in sweetener and vanilla, and enjoy!

Sunflower & Sesame Kefir

makes 1 quart

1 1/2 cup raw shelled sunflower seeds, soaked in 2 cups
water for 8 hours and rinsed
1/2 cup raw sesame seeds, soaked in 2 cups water for 8
hours and rinsed
3 cups purified water
2 Tbsp. Sucanat® (dehydrated sugar cane juice)
1 tsp. vanilla or 1/8 tsp. almond extract

1. Put soaked seeds in a blender with enough water to cover,
and purée until smooth and creamy. (Use as much or as little
water as necessary for desired consistency.)
2. Pour into a glass jar and cover with a clean towel. Put it in a
warm (not hot) place for 6 to 12 hours (depending upon
temperature and desired tartness) and allow to ferment.
3. Stir in sweetener and extract, and enjoy!

A luscious yogurt drink so rich and creamy, you'll think you've gone to heaven! Cultured nut and seed blends are good sources of protein and are rich in friendly flora, so they're good for your tummy. Make it at night and it'll be ready for you to enjoy in the morning!

*Guardian Angel,
please help me
have clarity of intent
so I can
focus my desires.*

You'll adore these creamy yogurts created from almonds and cashews. Enjoy them just as they are, or flavor them to suit your tastes. They are versatile and yummy! If you don't have a sprout bag, use a cheesecloth-lined colander.

Guardian Angel,
please help me
honor the Divinity
in all things.

Cashew Yogurt

makes 1 quart

2 cups raw cashews, soaked in purified water for 12 hours and drained
2 or more cups *Rejuvilac* (see pg. 15)
1/4 cup pure maple syrup (or, to taste)
1 tsp. vanilla extract or 1/8 tsp. almond extract

1. Place cashews in a blender with *Rejuvilac*. Blend until smooth and creamy, adding more *Rejuvilac*, if necessary.
2. Pour into a sprout bag and allow to drain for 1 to 2 hours.
3. Place in a warm (not hot) location and allow to ferment for another 8 to 12 hours.
4. Add syrup and extract to yogurt and blend well.
5. Pour yogurt into a glass jar and store in refrigerator.

Almond Yogurt

makes 1 quart

2 cups whole raw almonds, soaked in purified water for 24 hours, drained and peeled (see tips on peeling almonds, pg. 18)
2 or more cups purified water or *Rejuvilac* (see pg. 15)
1/4 cup pure maple syrup (or, to taste)
1 tsp. vanilla extract or 1/8 tsp. almond extract

1. Place soaked, peeled almonds in a blender with liquid. Blend until smooth and creamy, adding more liquid if necessary.
2. Pour into a sprout bag and allow to drain for 1 to 2 hours.
3. Place in a warm (not hot) location and allow to ferment for another 8 to 12 hours.
4. Add syrup and extract to yogurt and blend well.
5. Pour yogurt into a glass jar and store in refrigerator.

Sunflower Seed Yogurt

makes 1 quart

2 cups raw shelled sunflower seeds, soaked in purified
  water for 8 hours and drained
2 or more cups purified water
1/4 cup pure maple syrup (or, to taste)
1 tsp. vanilla extract or 1/8 tsp. almond extract

1. Place soaked sunflower seeds in a blender with water. Blend until smooth and creamy, adding more water if necessary.
2. Pour into a sprout bag and allow to drain for 1 to 2 hours.
3. Place in a warm (not hot) location and allow to ferment for another 8 to 12 hours.
4. Add syrup and extract to yogurt and blend well.
5. Pour yogurt into a glass jar and store in refrigerator.

Sunflower Sesame Seed Yogurt

makes 1 quart

1 1/2 cups raw shelled sunflower seeds, soaked in purified water for 8 hours and drained
1/2 cup raw sesame seeds, soaked in purified water for 8
  hours and drained
2 or more cups purified water
1/4 cups pure maple syrup (or, to taste)
1 tsp. vanilla extract or 1/8 tsp. almond extract

1. Place seeds in a blender with water. Blend until smooth.
2. Pour into a sprout bag and allow to drain for 1 to 2 hours.
3. Place in a warm (not hot) location and allow to ferment for another 8 to 12 hours.
4. Add syrup and extract to yogurt and blend well.
5. Pour yogurt into a glass jar and store in refrigerator.

These sensational non-dairy yogurts are thick and luscious, with a slightly tart sunflower or sunflower-sesame seed flavor. The longer you allow yogurt to ferment, the more the flavor changes, so taste it occasionally in order to create a taste that suits you.

Guardian Angel,
please help me
be accepting and
tolerant of others.

Creamy, soft, ricotta-like cheese is the result of culturing almond cream. It's remarkably versatile in spreads and fillings, and delightful when sweetened for use in desserts. It's well worth the time it takes to peel the almonds! (See pg. 18 for *Insights* on how to peel almonds.)

*Guardian Angel,
please help me
take the time to
enjoy the ordinary
pleasures of life.*

Almond Cheese

makes 2 cups

2 cups whole raw almonds, soaked in purified water for
    24 hours and drained
1 or more cups second or third day *Rejuvilac* (see pg. 15)

1. Remove skins from almonds and place in a blender. Add *Rejuvilac,* to cover. Blend until smooth and creamy, adding more *Rejuvilac,* if necessary, to keep the mixture blending.
2. Pour into a sprout bag or cheesecloth-lined colander and allow to drain for 1 to 2 hours.
3. Place in a warm (not hot) location and allow to ferment for another 7 to 10 hours. If a thick cheese is desired, place a clean weight on top of the cheese and allow it to continue draining. For a firmer texture, allow cheese to remain in the sprout bag or cheesecloth-lined colander after fermentation, then place it in the refrigerator for several more hours with a weight on top to allow additional whey to escape. Stored in an airtight container in the refrigerator, it will last for up to two weeks.
4. Season or sweeten *Almond Cheese* as desired before using. (See pg. 26, or check out *Angelic Appetizers & Sinful Spreads* for more great recipe ideas.)

Cashew Cream Cheese

makes 2 cups

2 1/2 cups raw cashews, soaked in purified water 12
  hours, rinsed and drained
1 or more cups second or third day *Rejuvilac* (see pg. 15)

1. Place cashews in a blender with *Rejuvilac,* to cover. Blend
   until smooth and creamy, adding only as much *Rejuvilac* as
   necessary to keep the mixture blending.
2. Pour into a sprout bag or cheesecloth-lined colander and
   allow to drain for 1 to 2 hours.
3. Place in a warm (not hot) location and allow to ferment for
   another 7 to 10 hours. If a thick cheese is desired, place a
   clean weight on top of the cheese and allow it to continue
   draining. For a firmer texture, allow cheese to remain in the
   sprout bag or cheesecloth-lined colander after fermentation,
   then place cheese in the refrigerator for several more hours
   with a weight on top to allow additional whey to escape. Stored
   in an airtight container in the refrigerator, it will last for up to
   two weeks.
4. Season or sweeten *Cashew Cheese* as desired before using.
   (See pg. 26, or check out *Angelic Appetizers & Sinful Spreads*
   for more great recipe ideas.)

Miracles do exist! This cream cheese is almost identical in flavor to Philadelphia® Cream Cheese and can be used in similar ways. In order to reap the rewards of the lactobacillus, cultured nut cheeses need to be enjoyed uncooked, but feel free to use them any way you want.

*Guardian Angel,
please help me
"lighten up" and
hold more Light.*

Sometimes, two seeds are better than one! This seed combination creates a whole new flavor and range of uses. It can be seasoned (see pg. 26) and used in spreads and dips, or sweetened for use in desserts. It is especially good in blender drinks, or enjoyed as a compliment to fruit.

Guardian Angel,
please help me
hold the feeling
of pure Love
in every moment.

Sunflower & Sesame Seed Cheese

makes 2 cups

1 1/2 cups raw shelled sunflower seeds, soaked in purified water 6 to 8 hours, rinsed and drained
1/2 cup raw sesame seeds, soaked in purified water 6–8 hours, rinsed and drained
1 or more cups purified or spring water

1. Place seeds in a blender with water. Blend until smooth and creamy, adding only as much water as necessary.
2. Pour into a sprout bag or cheesecloth-lined colander and allow to drain for 1 to 2 hours.
3. Place in a warm (not hot) location and allow to ferment for another 5 to 7 hours. If a thick cheese is desired, place a clean weight on top of the cheese and allow it to continue draining. For a firmer texture, allow cheese to remain in the sprout bag or cheesecloth-lined colander after fermentation, then place it in the refrigerator for several more hours with a weight on top to allow additional whey to escape. Stored in an airtight container in the refrigerator, it will last for up to one week.
4. Season or sweeten *Seed Cheese* as desired before using. (See pg. 26, or check out *Angelic Appetizers & Sinful Spreads* for more great recipe ideas.)

Chunky Cheese

makes 2 cups

1 cup raw almonds, soaked in purified water for 12 hours, rinsed and drained

1/2 cup raw shelled sunflower seeds, soaked in purified water for 6 to 8 hours, rinsed and drained

1/2 cup raw shelled pumpkin seeds, soaked in purified water for 6 to 8 hours, rinsed and drained

1 or more cups purified water

1. Combine the almonds and seeds together and hand mix. Place half of the mixture in a blender with water. Blend until smooth and creamy, adding only as much water as needed to keep the mixture blending. Add the remaining nuts and seeds and pulse chop. The mixture should be slightly chunky.

2. Pour into a sprout bag or cheesecloth-lined colander and allow to drain for 1 to 2 hours.

3. Place in a warm (not hot) location and allow to ferment for another 7 to 10 hours. If a thick cheese is desired, place a clean weight on top of the cheese and allow it to continue draining. For a firmer texture, allow cheese to remain in the sprout bag or cheesecloth-lined colander after fermentation, then place it in the refrigerator for several more hours with a weight on top to allow additional whey to escape. Stored in an airtight container in the refrigerator, it will keep for up to one week.

4. Season or sweeten *Chunky Cheese* as desired before using. (See pg. 26, or check out *Angelic Appetizers & Sinful Spreads* for more great recipe ideas.)

This nutty, textured cheese makes a great spread to use on *Multi-Grain Essene Bread* or *Sprouted Grain Crisps*. (See pgs. 138, 143.) Use your imagination and season it with chives, minced red onion with a hint of crushed garlic and herbs, curry powder and paprika, or crushed chili. This is guaranteed to be a favorite!

Guardian Angel,
please help me
let go of expectations
and be at peace
with what is.

There are infinite ways of using nut cheeses. Use your imagination to create any number of delightful dishes. This *Sweetened Cashew Cheese* is out of this world with fruit salads and desserts. Also, check out *Angelic Appetizers & Sinful Spreads* for incredible ways to use *Seasoned Almond Cheese*!

Guardian Angel,
please help me
see the light
of higher wisdom.

Seasoned Almond or Cashew Cheese

makes 2 cups

2 cups *Almond Cheese* or *Cashew Cheese* (see pg. 22, 23)
2 tsp. unpasteurized light miso paste
1 tsp. nutritional yeast
dash of nutmeg

1. Combine all ingredients and mix well. Use as a base for spreads (see *Angelic Appetizers & Sinful Spreads*), or as a binder in fillings. Will keep in an airtight container in the refrigerator for up to two weeks.

Sweetened Almond or Cashew Cheese

makes 2 cups

2 cups *Almond Cheese* or *Cashew Cheese* (see pg. 22, 23)
1/4–1/2 cup maple syrup or brown rice syrup
1 tsp. vanilla extract or 1/4 tsp. almond extract

1. Combine all ingredients and mix well. Use in desserts or with fruit salads. Sweetened nut cheeses will keep in an airtight container in the refrigerator for up to one week.

Seasoned Sunflower & Sesame Seed Cheese

makes 2 cups

2 cups *Sunflower & Sesame Seed Cheese* (see pg. 24)
2 tsp. unpasteurized light miso paste
1 tsp. nutritional yeast
dash of nutmeg

1. Combine all ingredients and mix well. Use as a base for spreads (see *Angelic Appetizers & Sinful Spreads*) or as a binder in fillings. Will keep in an airtight container in the refrigerator for up to two weeks.

Sweetened Sunflower & Sesame Seed Cheese

makes 2 cups

2 cups *Sunflower & Sesame Seed Cheese* (see pg. 24)
1/4–1/2 cup maple syrup or brown rice syrup
1 tsp. vanilla extract or 1/4 tsp. almond extract

1. Combine all ingredients and mix well. Use in desserts or with fruit salads. Sweetened seed cheeses will keep in an airtight container in the refrigerator for up to one week.

Here are two different ways of using seed cheeses. The flavor of these delicious, calcium- and protein-rich cultured foods can be varied in endless ways. Check out *Angelic Appetizers & Sinful Spreads* for some taste-pleasing recipes!

Guardian Angel, please help me fully express my love energy.

Almond cheese makes a perfect dairy-free ricotta. To reap the benefits of acidophilus, use it in uncooked recipes. Cooked, it will respond much like regular ricotta cheese.

Guardian Angel,
please help me
allow Divine Love
to flow through me.

Almond Ricotta Cheese

makes 1 cup

3/4 cup firm *Almond Cheese* (see pg. 22)
1/4 cup red onion, minced
1 Tbsp. light miso
1/2 Tbsp. nutritional yeast
1/2 small clove garlic, crushed
dash of nutmeg
dash of white pepper

1. Combine ingredients, adding water if needed to achieve desired consistency. Can be stored in refrigerator for up to one week. Serve as a spread for *Multi-Grain Essene Bread* (see pg. 138), *Sprouted Grain Crisps* (see pg. 143), or as a dip for fresh vegetables.

Note: Cheese will thicken as it sits. More water may be needed after storing it in the refrigerator.

Almond Feta-ish Cheese

makes 1 cup

3/4 cup very firm *Almond Cheese* (see pg. 22)
1 Tbsp. light miso
1/2 Tbsp. nutritional yeast
1/2 small clove garlic, crushed
1/2 tsp. lemon juice
1/2 tsp. sea salt (or, to taste)
dash of nutmeg
dash of white pepper
1/2 tsp. psyllium powder (optional; use if cheese is not
    firm)

1. Combine ingredients for cheese and mix well. Spoon into a
    cheesecloth-lined, plastic berry basket or colander and place
    a weight on top. (A plastic bag filled with beans works well.)
    Allow to remain in refrigerator another 12 hours. Use in
    salads and other recipes that call for feta cheese.

I love Greek salads and always missed the feta cheese in my non-dairy versions. So, when I came up with this almond feta, I was delighted! Make it a day or two ahead, so it has plenty of time to release its whey and become firm.

*Guardian Angel,
please help me
love myself
more.*

No wonder this enzyme-rich food is reputed to be responsible for the long lives of so many healthy elders. It aids in the growth of new cells and is a very cleansing food. It's easy to make and tastes great, but start with small amounts at first. It's a great detoxifier, so a little is good, but a lot may not be better!

Guardian Angel,
please help me
see my Light
reflected in others.

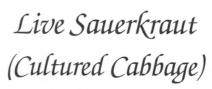

Live Sauerkraut (Cultured Cabbage)

makes 1 quart

1 medium-size cabbage, finely shredded or ground
    (reserve several outer leaves and pieces of cabbage to
    cover sauerkraut)
1/2 tsp. sea salt (optional)

1. Firmly pack finely shredded cabbage into a deep glass bowl or crock. (The cabbage should be very juicy. If not, pound on it with a heavy weight or grind it a little finer to release the juices.)
2. Place the reserved leaves over the top, allowing them to extend partially up the side of the crock; put a small saucer on top.
3. Fill a clean plastic bag with grains or beans to act as a weight and place it on top of the saucer. Allow some space around the sides to ensure a good air supply.
4. Cover the top with a clean dish towel.
5. Place in a temperate, dark closet for 3 to 4 days. (It will ferment sooner in warmer weather.)
6. Store your kraut in a glass jar in the refrigerator. It will last two weeks or more, but is best eaten as soon as possible to ensure live lactobacillus bacteria.

Kim Chee
(Spicy Korean Cultured Cabbage)
makes 1 1/2 quarts

1 medium-size cabbage, finely shredded or ground
   (reserve several outer leaves and pieces of cabbage to
   cover *Kim Chee*)
1 daikon radish, finely shredded or ground
1/4 cup red onion, minced
1 clove garlic, crushed
1 Tbsp. grated fresh ginger root
1/2 tsp. sea salt
1/8 tsp. cayenne pepper

1. Combine all ingredients and firmly pack into a deep glass
   bowl or crock. (The cabbage should be very juicy; if not,
   pound on it with a heavy weight or grind it a little finer to
   release the juices.)
2. Place the reserved leaves over the top, allowing them to extend partially up the side of the crock; put a small saucer on
   top.
3. Fill a clean plastic bag with grains or beans to act as a weight
   and place it on top of the saucer. Allow some space around
   the sides to ensure a good air supply.
4. Cover the top with a clean dish towel.
5. Place in a temperate, dark closet for 3 to 4 days. (It will
   ferment sooner in warmer weather.)
6. Store your *Kim Chee* in a glass jar in the refrigerator. It will
   last two weeks or more, but is best eaten as soon as possible
   to ensure live lactobacillus bacteria.

If you like spicy, pungent foods, you'll love this Korean version of sauerkraut. Alter the flavor by adding different kinds of chilies, more fresh ginger, garlic, green onions, or whatever you like! Also try using Asian (Napa) cabbage instead of head cabbage. Enjoy *Kim Chee* as a condiment or garnish—it'll liven up any meal!

*Guardian Angel,
please help me
develop a peaceful,
quiet mind.*

Slightly milder and sweeter in flavor, this kraut is a feast for the eyes! You can use almost any vegetables you like, including celery, broccoli, radish, or onion. Also, if you prefer, you may choose purple cabbage or Asian (Napa) cabbage. Seasonings can vary with your mood—so, be creative!

Guardian Angel,
please help me
remember to breathe
the breath of life
consciously and deeply.

Vegekraut
(Cultured Mixed Vegetables)

makes 1 1/2 quarts

1 medium-size cabbage, finely shredded or ground
    (reserve several outer leaves and pieces of cabbage to
    cover *Vegekraut*)
1 beet, trimmed and finely shredded or ground
2 carrots, finely shredded or ground
1/2 tsp. dill weed or caraway
1/4 tsp. ground celery seed
1/4 tsp. dulse or kelp powder
1/4 tsp. sea salt

1. Combine ingredients and mix well. Firmly pack into a deep glass bowl or crock. (The cabbage should be very juicy. If not, pound on it with a heavy weight or grind it a little finer to release the juices.)
2. Place the reserved leaves over the top, allowing them to extend partially up the side of the crock; put a small saucer on top.
3. Fill a clean plastic bag with grains or beans to act as a weight and place it on top of the saucer. Allow some space around the sides to ensure a good air supply.
4. Cover the top with a clean dish towel.
5. Place in a temperate, dark closet for 3 to 4 days. (It will ferment sooner in warmer weather.)
6. Store your *Vegekraut* in a glass jar in the refrigerator. It will last two weeks or more, but is best eaten as soon as possible to ensure live lactobacillus bacteria.

Applekraut
(Cultured Cabbage with Apples)

makes 1–1 1/2 quarts

1 medium-size cabbage, finely shredded or ground
  (reserve several outer leaves and pieces of cabbage to
  cover *Applekraut*)
2 tart, firm apples, peeled, cored, and shredded
1 tsp. freshly grated ginger root

1. Combine ingredients and mix well. Firmly pack into a deep glass bowl or crock. (The cabbage should be very juicy. If not, pound on it with a heavy weight or grind it a little finer to release the juices.)
2. Place the reserved leaves over the top, allowing them to extend partially up the side of the crock; put a small saucer on top.
3. Fill a clean plastic bag with grains or beans to act as a weight and place it on top of the saucer. Allow some space around the sides to ensure a good air supply.
4. Cover the top with a clean dish towel.
5. Place in a temperate, dark closet for 3 to 4 days. (It will ferment sooner in warmer weather.)
6. Store your *Applekraut* in a glass jar in the refrigerator. It will last two weeks or more, but is best eaten soon to insure live lactobacillus bacteria.

This kraut is sensational! The apple and ginger create a wonderful combination of sweetness and tang. For variety, add spices such as anise seed, curry powder, caraway, or cardamom. These krauts are easy to make and very health promoting. Use your imagination and see how many great flavors you can create!

*Guardian Angel,
please help me
slow down and
trust what is.*

Chapter Four

Bountiful Fruits

A Talk with Spirit about Abundance:

Dear One, please help me accept that The Universe supports me in creating a life of joy and abundance. I ask that the fruits of life surround me in all their forms, providing health, right livelihood, financial security, unconditional love, and peace of mind. I need assurance that I will be rewarded for following my heart and trusting Divine Guidance to light my path. I ask all energies of Light and Love to assist me in holding only positive thoughts concerning my ability to create a life of health, prosperity, and fulfillment.

I am divinely grateful for these gifts of Light, which have been lovingly provided for my nourishment and which I recognize as a symbol of abundance. I respect and give thanks to these foods for their energy and generosity. I love you, I bless you, I am one with you and All That Is.

Recipes at a Glance

Bountiful Fruits

The angels couldn't be more delighted with this beautiful array of tantalizing seasonal fruits. It's a wonderful way to begin the day! If you wish, serve them with your choice of sweetened *Cashew* or *Almond Yogurt*.

Guardian Angel, please help me recognize the sacredness in everything I do.

Country Fruit Platter

serves 4

2 apples, quartered lengthwise and cored
2 pears, quartered lengthwise and cored
2 peaches, quartered lengthwise, pits removed
4 plums, cut in half, pits removed
4 apricots, cut in half, pits removed
1 pint cherries
1 pint blueberries or blackberries
sweetened *Cashew* or *Almond Yogurt* (see pg. 20)

1. Arrange fruit attractively on a platter, either scattering the berries over the top, or placing them in small dishes on the platter. Serve with sweetened *Cashew* or *Almond Yogurt* on the side.

Tropical Fruit Platter

serves 4

2 papayas, peeled, seeded, and quartered lengthwise
1/2 pineapple, peeled, cored, and cut into spears
2 bananas, peeled and cut into thirds
2 mangos, peeled and sliced
4 guavas, peeled and cut in halves
3 mandarin oranges, peeled and sectioned into quarters
4 kiwi fruit, peeled and cut into halves
juice of 1 lime
1/2 coconut, peeled and shredded (for garnish)

1. Arrange fruit attractively on a platter and drizzle lime over the papaya and mango.
2. Sprinkle coconut over the top and serve immediately.

Hawaiian Sunrise Salad

serves 4

2 medium papayas, peeled, seeded, and chopped
1/2 pineapple, peeled, cored, and chopped
2 mangos, peeled, pitted, and chopped
2 ripe bananas, peeled and sliced
2 oranges, peeled, broken into sections, and
    cut into pieces
2 kiwi fruit, peeled, quartered lengthwise, and sliced
juice of 1 lime

1. Combine all ingredients together, toss, and serve at once.

Pacific Isles Pineapple Boat

serves 4

1 pineapple
2 bananas, peeled and sliced.
1/2 cherimoya, peeled, seeded, and chopped
2 guavas, peeled, seeded, and chopped
1 papaya, peeled, seeded, and chopped
1 mango, peeled and chopped
juice of one lime

1. Slice pineapple lengthwise. Cut pineapple around the outer edge, leaving a firm shell. Remove the fruit, discard the core, and chop. Reserve shell to use as a bowl for the salad.
2. Combine chopped pineapple with remaining fruit and toss. Serve in pineapple shell as is, or with *Almond* or *Cashew Yogurt*. (See pg. 20)

You can almost hear the angels singing when you prepare these light-filled tropical salads! Guests and family members will think they're on a Hawaiian cruise!

*Guardian Angel,
please help me
illuminate
the inner regions
of my soul.*

There's nothing like sweet, fresh berries to delight your senses. This is what spring is all about! Anyone who loves citrus fruit will delight in this lively citrus salad.

Guardian Angel, please help me become a vessel of Divine Light.

Mountain Berry Salad

serves 4

1/2 pint raspberries or salmonberries
1/2 pint blackberries or boysenberries
1/2 pint blueberries or huckleberries
1/2 pint strawberries
1/2 pint currents or gooseberries
1/2 cup sweetened *Almond* or *Cashew Yogurt*
   (See pg. 20)

1. Combine all berries together and toss gently. Serve in individual bowls and top with sweetened *Almond* or *Cashew Yogurt*.

Santa Barbara Citrus Salad

serves 4

2 navel oranges, peeled and cut into wheels
3 mandarin oranges, peeled and cut into wheels
3 tangerines, peeled and cut into wheels
2 grapefruit, peeled and sectioned, removing outer skins
1 pomegranate, separate seeds from shell and skin
   (use seeds only)
1 cup kumquats, cut into halves
1/2 cup orange juice

1. Toss ingredients together and serve.

California's Best Fruit Salad

serves 4

4 mandarin oranges or tangerines, peeled and chopped
1 grapefruit, peeled and chopped
2 Asian pears, cored and chopped
8 fresh figs, chopped
4 kiwi, peeled and chopped
2 cups grapes, separated from stems
1 persimmon, skinned, seeded, and puréed
juice of 1 lime
seeds of 1 pomegranate
4 mint sprigs

1. Combine first 6 ingredients and toss gently.
2. Combine lime juice and persimmon together and mix well.
3. Place fruit salad on individual plates and spoon persimmon mixture in center of each. Garnish with pomegranate seeds and mint and serve immediately.

Winter Fruit Salad

serves 4

8 dried figs, soaked overnight and chopped
1/2 cup raisins or currents, soaked overnight
4 dried apricots, soaked overnight and chopped
4 prunes, soaked overnight, pitted and quartered
2 fresh apples, cored and chopped
juice of 1 lime

1. Combine ingredients together and toss gently. If desired, serve with *Almond* or *Cashew Yogurt* (see pg. 20).

One of the the best things about California is the avail ability of fresh fruits. This is an extra special fruit salad that uses many of the unique fruits that grow there.

Even when fresh fruit isn't available, you can still enjoy the precious gift of fruit in the morning. This winter salad is convenient and delicious!

*Guardian Angel,
please help me
develop a conscious
perception of
the Angelic Realms.*

Either of these delightful fruit recipes would make an elegant first course for breakfast or brunch. There is something really exquisite about strawberries and cream that can not be described with words! The closest I can come to it is, luscious!

Guardian Angel,
please help me
radiate strength
and Light.

Peaches with Strawberry Melon Coulis

serves 4

1/4 melon of choice, peeled, seeded, and puréed
2 cups ripe strawberries, cleaned, trimmed, and puréed
4 large peaches, pitted and sliced

1. Spoon 1/4 of each purée onto individual plates to form a pleasant design.
2. Fan peach slices on top of purées and serve immediately.

Strawberries 'n Cashew Cream

serves 4

2 pints ripe strawberries, trimmed, drained well, and sliced in half lengthwise
1 cup sweetened *Cashew Cream* (see pg. 17)
4 sprigs fresh mint

1. Gently toss strawberries and sweetened *Cashew Cream*, reserving 4 strawberry halves to use as garnish.
2. Spoon strawberry mixture into individual serving dishes and garnish with a strawberry half and mint. Serve immediately.

Mexican Fruit Skewers

serves 3–4

1 medium jicama, peeled and cut into 1-inch chunks
2 bananas, sliced into 1-inch rounds
1 firm papaya, peeled, seeded, and cut into 1-inch pieces
2 firm mangos, peeled and cut into 1-inch pieces
2 oranges, peeled and cut into 1-inch pieces
1 pint strawberries, washed and trimmed
juice of 1 lime
ground red pepper (optional)

1. Arrange the fruit by color on long bamboo skewers.
2. Squeeze lime over fruits and sprinkle very lightly with red pepper just before serving.

Danish Fruit Soup

serves 4

16 fresh apricots, pitted
2 cups strawberries, cleaned and trimmed
2 cups fresh squeezed orange juice

1. Combine ingredients in a blender and purée.
2. Strain mixture and serve chilled or at room temperature.

Both of these recipes are fun and unusual ways to serve fruit, and a great way to get finicky children to eat! You can serve this wonderful gourmet soup as a prelude to breakfast or brunch. It's easy to prepare, yet creative and delicious! Vary the fruits according to what's in season.

Guardian Angel,
please help me
see each moment as
a sacred gift.

These incredibly delicious smoothies are a great way to start your day. Use any fresh seasonal fruit and be creative. You can't make a bad smoothie!

Guardian Angel,
please help me
fill my life with
acts of kindness.

Melon Smoothie

serves 2–3

1 cantaloupe or honeydew, peeled, seeded, and chopped
1 cup fresh orange juice or purified water

1. Purée fruit and juice in a blender and enjoy!

Mango Smoothie

serves 2

2 fresh mangos, peeled and seeded
2 cups fresh orange juice or apple juice

1. Purée fruit and juice in a blender and enjoy!

Banana Nectarine Smoothie

serves 2

3 nectarines, pitted
3 bananas, peeled
3 cups fresh orange or apple juice

1. Purée fruit and juice in a blender and enjoy!

Papaya Banana Smoothie

serves 2

1 papaya, peeled and seeded
3 bananas, peeled
3 cups fresh orange or grapefruit juice

1. Purée fruit and juice in a blender and enjoy!

Apple Banana Berry Smoothie

serves 2

1 pint berries of choice, cleaned and trimmed
2 bananas, peeled
2 cups fresh apple juice

1. Purée fruit and juice in a blender and enjoy!

Carob Banana Almond Shake

serves 2

1 cup soaked almonds
2 cups water
3 large bananas
1–2 Tbsp. carob powder

1. Purée ingredients in a blender until smooth and enjoy!

Smoothies and shakes are great for breakfast or snacks. Here are two more delectable smoothies and a shake creation. Also try papaya, kiwi, cherimoya, apricot, peach, pear, or whatever makes your tummy sing!

*Guardian Angel,
please help me
see the Light
in everyone.*

If you don't tell, they'll never know just how simple and nutritious these delicious breakfast puddings are! The dehydrated fruits create a surprising gelatinous effect.

Guardian Angel,
please help me be
more angelic in
my daily thoughts
and deeds.

Banana Surprise Breakfast Pudding

serves 2

8 large prunes, soaked overnight, drained, and pitted
3 ripe bananas, peeled

1. Combine in a blender and purée until smooth and creamy.
2. If possible, allow to chill for one hour before serving.

Apple Apricot Breakfast Pudding

serves 2

12 dehydrated apricot halves, soaked overnight and drained
2 apples, seeded and chopped
1/2 tsp. ground cinnamon or ground ginger

1. Combine ingredients in a food processor, or blender, and purée until smooth. (If using a blender, separate mixture in half.)
2. If possible, allow to chill for one hour before serving.

Baked Bananas with Cinnamon

serves 4

8–10 almost ripe bananas, peeled, and cut lengthwise
1/2 cup Sucanat® (dehydrated sugar cane juice)
1 tsp. cinnamon
1 cup coconut milk or sweetened *Cashew Cream* (see pg. 17)

1. Lay half the bananas in a shallow baking dish and sprinkle with half the Sucanat®. Dust the top evenly with half the cinnamon. Repeat, using remaining ingredients.
2. Bake in an oiled baking dish at 375 degrees for 30 minutes.
3. Allow bananas to cool. Meanwhile, gently warm coconut milk or sweetened *Cashew Cream*.
4. Serve topped with warm coconut milk or sweetened *Cashew Cream*.

Baked Spiced Apples

serves 4

4 large green apples, cored and quartered
1 tsp. cinnamon
1/2 tsp. each allspice and ground ginger
1/4 tsp. nutmeg
1/2 cup Sucanat® (dehydrated sugar cane juice)
1 cup sweetened *Cashew Cream*. (see pg. 17)

1. Combine ingredients, except *Cashew Cream*, and toss well.
2. Bake in a shallow, oiled baking dish at 375 degrees for 30 to 45 minutes.
3. Allow apples to cool. Meanwhile, gently warm cream.
4. Serve topped with warm sweetened *Cashew Cream*.

If you want your kitchen to smell like heaven, this will do it! Warm and nurturing on cold days, these delectable dishes are great for breakfasts as snacks, or even as desserts.

Guardian Angel, please help me see God in everyone and everything.

It's worth the investment in a dehydrator just to make fruit leathers! Try different kinds of fruit or fruit combos and discover your favorites! Or, roll banana leather around nut butter for an incredible treat!

Guardian Angel,
please help me become
a shining presence
for all to see.

Banana Leather

1 1/2–2 bananas per dehydrator sheet

1. Peel bananas and liquefy in a blender or food processor.
2. Spread banana blend on a plastic dehydrator sheet using approximately 1 cup of mixture to form a square 1/4 inch thick.
3. Dehydrate (no hotter than 118 degrees) for 12 to 24 hours. Vary drying time to achieve desired firmness. (Should be slightly tacky, not sticky or overly crisp.)
4. Remove from sheet and roll into cylinder for easy storage. Will keep for several months.

Banana Cashew Roll-ups

makes 48 bite-size pieces

6 sheets banana leather (see recipe above)
1 1/2 cup *Cashew Butter* (see pg. 68)

1. Spread 1/4 cup fresh cashew butter on the bottom third of each sheet of banana leather and roll tightly, jelly-roll style.
2. Slice each roll into eight rounds. Stored in an airtight container in the refrigerator, they will keep for up to one month.

Apricot Leather

6–8 sweet, ripe apricots per sheet

1. Liquefy apricots in blender or food processor.
2. Spread apricot purée on a plastic dehydrator sheet using approximately 1 cup of mixture to form a square 1/4 inch thick.
3. Dehydrate (no hotter than 118 degrees) for 12 to 24 hours. Vary drying time to achieve desired firmness. (Should be slightly tacky, not sticky or overly crisp.)
4. Remove from sheet and roll into a cylinder for easy storage. Will keep for several months.

Apricot Fig Roll-ups

makes 48 bite-size pieces

6 sheets *Apricot Leather* (see recipe above)

Filling:
12 dehydrated figs, ground
1 cup shredded coconut (optional)
1/2 cup firm *Almond* or *Cashew Cheese* (see pg. 22, 23)

1. Combine filling ingredients together and purée in food processor. Spread 1/4 cup of mixture on the bottom third of each sheet of apricot leather and roll tightly, jelly-roll style.
2. Slice each roll into eight rounds. Stored in an airtight container, it will keep in the refrigerator for up to 1 week. (For longer storage time, substitute *Cashew Butter* (see pg. 68) for *Almond* or *Cashew Cheese*.)

If you buy fruit in high season, you'll be able to make these incredible snacks for just pennies. Roll them up for a great lunchbox treat, or get creative with fillings to make them extra special!

*Guardian Angel,
please help me
master my thinking
and live in my heart.*

How easy can it be to make incredible "ice cream"!? This is delicious and nutritious and makes a great afternoon snack or dessert. If you prefer, you can substitute carob powder for chocolate.

*Guardian Angel,
please help me be
balanced in mind, body
and spirit.*

Bananas! I Scream, with Chocolate Sauce

1–2 ripe bananas per serving, peeled and sliced into
   1/2– inch rounds

1. Line a cookie sheet with plastic wrap and arrange banana slices in a single layer on top. Cover with plastic wrap and freeze.
2. Place frozen banana slices in food processor and purée until mixture forms a smooth, solid clump of *Bananas! I Scream*. Or, use a Champion Juicer® to make soft serve ice cream, as makers recommend, using the blank filter and homogenizing. If necessary, return to refrigerator for up to 4 hours before serving.

Chocolate Sauce

makes 3/4 cup

1/2 cup unsweetened chocolate powder
1/2 cup liquid mixed fruit sweetener (Mystic Lakes®)
1 tsp. vanilla extract

1. Blend all ingredients together until smooth. Can be stored in refrigerator for up to three months.

Variations:

Carob Sauce – Use untoasted carob powder instead of chocolate and replace with 1/4–1/3 cup sweetener.

Mocha Sauce – Substitute 2 Tbsp. Roma® (powdered grain beverage) for chocolate, or carob for a "mocha" taste.

Mangos! I Scream

1–2 ripe mangos per serving, peeled and sliced

1. Line a cookie sheet with plastic wrap and arrange mango slices on top in a single layer. Cover with plastic wrap and freeze.
2. Place frozen mango slices in food processor and purée until mixture forms a smooth, solid clump of *Mangos! I Scream*. Or, use a Champion Juicer® to make soft serve ice cream, as makers recommend, utilizing the blank filter and homogenizing. If necessary, return to refrigerator for up to 4 hours prior to serving.

Fruit Sherbet

makes 1 quart

1 cup raw unsalted cashews, soaked in 1 cup water
1 1/2 cups fresh ripe fruit of choice, peeled and seeded

1. Rinse and drain cashews and put in blender with just enough water to keep the mixture blending. Purée until smooth and creamy. If it's not perfectly smooth, process longer or strain through fine cheesecloth.
2. Add fruit to cashew cream in blender and purée until smooth.
3. Pour mixture into ice cube trays and freeze until firm.
4. Prior to serving, remove from freezer and whip in food processor until fluffy. Return to freezer until serving time.

You'll be amazed when you taste these heavenly treats! It's hard to believe they're so easy to make! Use your favorite seasonal fruits to create other wonderful ice creams and sherbets for those hot summer days.

*Guardian Angel,
please help me trust
your guidance and
recognize Truth.*

I always love it in fine restaurants when sorbets are served between courses. They cleanse the palate and really set the meal apart as something special!

A sorbet or ice can be enjoyed as an afternoon snack, or served as an elegant addition to any meal—especially when presented in small wine glasses.

*Guardian Angel,
please help me know
that God exists
in everyone
and everything.*

French Champagne-Berry Ice

serves 4

2 cups blackberries, rinsed and drained
2 cups raspberries, rinsed and drained
1/2 cup FruitSource® or granulated fructose (or more, if berries are tart)
1 Tbsp. lime juice
1/2 cup purified water
1 1/2 cups Champagne (divided use)

1. Combine berries, FruitSource®, water, and lime juice in a large pot and bring to a boil. Reduce heat and simmer for 3 to 4 minutes.
2. Meanwhile, in a small pot, bring 1 cup of champagne to a boil. Remove from heat and allow to cool. (The alcohol must be allowed to escape through boiling or it will inhibit freezing.)
3. Purée berry mixture in a blender or food processor until smooth. Add boiled champagne and blend. Pour mixture through a sieve into a bowl to remove seeds. (Discard seeds.)
5. Freeze sorbet in ice cube trays until solid. Remove from freezer and purée in a blender or food processor until slushy. Serve at once, or return to freezer for a couple of hours, until serving time.
6. Form small spoonfuls and place them in individual champagne glasses. If desired, pour remaining active champagne over the top and serve.

Hawaiian Pineapple Sorbet

serves 4

4 cups fresh pineapple, peeled, cored, and chopped
1 1/2 cups fresh pineapple juice
1 banana, peeled
juice of 1 lime

1. Purée ingredients and pour into ice cube trays. Freeze 12 hours or longer.
2. Before serving, remove from ice cube trays and place in a food processor.
3. Purée and serve immediately, or return to refrigerator for up to 4 hours.

Sensational Strawberry Sorbet

serves 4

4 cups strawberries, cleaned and trimmed
1 1/2 cups fresh orange juice
1 banana, peeled

1. Purée ingredients and pour into ice cube trays. Freeze 12 hours or longer.
2. Before serving, remove from ice cube trays and place in a food processor.
3. Purée and serve immediately, or return to refrigerator for up to 4 hours.

These are two of my favorite flavors of sorbet. They're both smooth, creamy, and refreshing! Use these basic recipes to create any flavor you desire. Simply replace the pineapple with whatever delights your taste buds.

Guardian Angel,
please help me allow
your Divine Love to
transform me into
Light and Love.

Chapter Five

Angelic Appetizers & Sinful Spreads

A Talk with Spirit about Acceptance

I ask Divine guidance to assist me in loving and accepting myself as I am. I know that every experience I've had in my life has brought me to this moment; therefore, I bless my past and all who have participated in creating me as I am today. Help me understand that each part of me is a Divine piece of the whole. Help me to be grateful to my body for providing me with a comfortable home and to my mind for the wisdom to desire a balanced life. I ask for your assistance so that I may love myself, accept who I am, and express my true self without fear of rejection or loss of love. Help me also accept others for who they are without expectation of how they "should" be.

I recognize that we are all one and that these foods, like myself, are perfect examples of God in nature. Therefore, I glorify them and see them as Divine, just as I am Divine. As we unite, our Light becomes even more bright. I love you, I bless you, I am one with you and All That Is.

Recipes at a Glance

Angelic Appetizers

Sinful Spreads

I used to love the smell of chilies and tomatoes roasting, as I watched my Mexican grand-mother making fresh salsa. I don't use a stone mortar to crush the mixture as she did, but the recipe has the same simple elegance.

*Guardian Angel,
please help me practice
loving kindness
in everything I do.*

Mexican Tomato Salsa

serves 6

4 medium tomatoes
2 small serrano chilies
2 green onions, thinly sliced
2 whole long green (Anaheim) chilies
1 clove garlic, crushed
2 Tbsp. cilantro leaves (Chinese parsley), minced
1/4 tsp. sea salt (or, to taste)

1. Place tomatoes and chilies on baking sheet and roast under oven broiler, turning, just until skin is scorched and blistered, about 5 minutes.
2. Allow tomatoes and peppers to cool slightly, then peel, stem, seed, and dice. (See *Insights* below)
3. Combine all ingredients and mix well. Allow to mellow at least 15 minutes before serving. The flavor will improve with time.

Insights: To seed tomatoes, cut them in half lengthwise, from top to bottom. Using a sharp paring knife, slice a semicircle around the bottom of the cut side connecting the two seed cavities. Lift the tomato pulp up and out of the way to remove the seeds. You may retain the seeds and juice to use in fresh juices, or give it to your canine companion.

Thai
Spicy Cucumber Condiment

makes 2 cups

1 firm cucumber, peeled, cut in half lengthwise, and
    seeded
2 Tbsp. lime juice or rice vinegar
2 Tbsp. brown rice syrup
1 tsp. sea salt
1/4 tsp. white pepper
1/2 small red onion, julienned
1 fresh hot red chili, seeded and cut into thin slivers,
    1/4-inch long

1. Slice the cucumber crosswise as thin as possible.
2. Toss all ingredients together thoroughly and serve at once
   or keep in an airtight container in the refrigerator for no
   more than a few hours.
3. Serve with *Sea Vegetable Grain Crisps* (see pg. 143).

Insights: To julienne an onion, remove the outer skins
and cut it in half, from top to root. With the cut side down,
slice it lengthwise, following the natural lines and contour
of the onion to form long, thin, julienne slices. Cutting the
onion crosswise will create half circles.

This traditional Southeast Asian appetizer will wake up your taste buds! Vary the seasonings to suit your palate. In Thailand, it's hot, hotter and hottest!

Guardian Angel,
please help me
experience
emotional calm and
inner peace.

Japanese Chilled Noodle Appetizer

serves 4

This Japanese-inspired first course is simple, yet fragrant and delicious. It also makes a great lunch or dinner, served with *Sunomono* or *Japanese Sushimaki*. (See pg. 87, 166)

Guardian Angel, please help me be willing to listen and learn from everyone.

8 ounces somen noodles

Japanese Dipping Sauce:
1 cup *Shiitake Dashi* (see pg. 133)
1/4 cup Aji Mirin® sweet rice wine
1/4 cup tamari soy sauce
2 green onions, thinly sliced
1 tsp. fresh ginger root, peeled, minced, and finely grated
1/2 tsp. toasted sesame oil
pinch of assorted chili pepper seasoning

1 tsp. roasted sesame seeds

1. Cook noodles according to directions on the package and store in ice water until ready to serve.
2. Combine ingredients for dipping sauce, and chill.
3. Just before serving, drain noodles and divide into small individual dishes. Garnish with sesame seeds, and serve the chilled dipping sauce on the side.

Insights: Fresh ginger root is used extensively in Asian and Middle Eastern cuisine and is reputed to be an excellent digestive aid. To keep it handy, peel and freeze it, then shred as needed without defrosting. Fresh ginger is also wonderful in fresh fruit, vegetable juices, and herbal teas. A little goes a long way, so use it sparingly.

Antipasto
(Sicilian Appetizer Tray)
serves 4

Italian Vinaigrette:
2 Tbsp. flax oil or extra-virgin olive oil
2 Tbsp. lime juice or balsamic vinegar
2 Tbsp. water
1 clove garlic, crushed
1/2 tsp. Italian seasoning
1 Tbsp. fresh parsley, minced
1/2 tsp. Vege-Sal® or sea salt (or, to taste)

12 whole mushrooms, trimmed and lightly steamed
12 spears of asparagus, trimmed and lightly steamed
1 cup cauliflower, broken into florets and lightly steamed
1 cup broccoli, broken into florets and lightly steamed
1 medium zucchini, sliced into rounds and lightly
   steamed
1 sweet red pepper, roasted, peeled, and seeded
1 yellow bell pepper, roasted, peeled, and seeded
1 green bell pepper, roasted, peeled, and seeded
8–12 small, cooked artichoke hearts

1. Combine ingredients for *Vinaigrette* and allow to mellow for at least 30 minutes while preparing the vegetables.
2. Steam mushrooms, asparagus, broccoli, cauliflower, and zucchini for a few minutes, and rinse in ice water.
3. Slice roasted peppers into quarters lengthwise and roll from wide end to narrow end.
4. Arrange the vegetables attractively on a platter and pour the *Vinaigrette* evenly over the top.
5. Allow to marinate for at least 1/2 hour prior to serving. Serve at room temperature.

I usualy serve this traditional Italian appetizer mostly raw, but in this version we lightly steam and marinate the vegetables as they do in Sicily. Serve it with *Black Olive Tapinade* and *Sprouted Grain Crisps.* (See pg. 75, 143)

Guardian Angel, please help me become a source of helpfulness and Light to all.

Fragrant and delicious, these little packages of seasoned rice are a specialty of Greece and of the Arabic Mediterranean. They are wonderful served warm or cold.

*Guardian Angel,
please help me
remain on the path to
personal freedom.*

Dolmas

(Greek Seasoned Rice in Grape Leaves)

serves 6 (36–40 pieces)

Filling:
3/4 cup medium-grain brown rice, washed and drained
1 1/4 cup purified water
1 tsp. sea salt (divided use)
1 cup (well packed) Italian parsley, minced
4 scallions, finely sliced
1/4 cup pine nuts, chopped
freshly ground pepper (to taste)

1 pound jar prepared grape leaves
boiling water

Sauce:
1/4 cup lemon juice
1 tsp. brown rice syrup
3 cloves garlic, crushed
1/2 tsp. salt
1 1/2 cup purified water

1. Place rice, 1 1/4 cup water, and 1/2 tsp. salt in pot and bring to a boil. Cover and reduce heat to low. Simmer for 50 minutes until all moisture is absorbed. Remove from heat and allow to sit, covered, for another 10 minutes. (Do not stir!)

2. Meanwhile, carefully remove grape leaves from jar and separate. Place in colander and rinse well. Put them in a large bowl and pour boiling water over them. Drain and rinse again. Separate and flatten on a clean towel. Put broken leaves aside and reserve.

3. Combine rice and remaining filling ingredients together in a bowl and mix.

4. Line a deep skillet or wide pot with a layer of the broken grape leaves.

5. Begin stuffing the flattened grape leaves: lay one down in front of you, shiny side down, with the stem end nearest you. Place a heaping teaspoon of filling in the center of the leaf, near the stem end. Fold the stem end over the filling. Then holding it in place, fold the left and right sides in over the filling. From the folded stem end, tightly roll the leaf away from you, toward the tip. Continue until all *Dolmas* are completed.

6. Lay *Dolmas* seam side down and crowd tightly together in the leaf-lined pot. If necessary, form a second layer.

7. Mix sauce ingredients together and pour over the *Dolmas*.

8. Bring to a boil. Cover, reduce heat to low, and simmer 30 minutes, checking occasionally to insure they do not dry out.

9. Cool to room temperature before serving.

Flat leafed (Italian) parsley has an astringently sweet flavor and is especially good in *Dolmas*. All parsley needs to be washed well to remove any sand that may elude your detection.

Guardian Angel, please help me develop a conscious perception of the Heavenly Spheres.

For this delectable and very unusual recipe, only the most delicate, edible portion of the artichoke is prepared, so there are no messy leaves for guests to struggle with. It is wonderful as an appetizer or a side dish!

Guardian Angel,
please give me the
patience to allow
myself to unfold
in my own time.

Italian
Grilled Artichoke Hearts
serves 4

4 medium artichokes
juice of 1 lemon in 2 cups water
4 cloves garlic, sliced
olive oil cooking spray or 1/2 tsp. olive oil

1. Remove all of the tough outer leaves from the artichokes, leaving only the most tender leaves. Trim and peel the stem using a sharp knife. Cut off the top half of the leaves and discard. Slice each artichoke lengthwise into 8 equal parts and remove the choke. Place them in the lemon water until ready to cook. (Outer leaves may be reserved for later use.)
2. Heat a non-stick skillet to medium and season with oil. Sauté the artichokes and garlic for 5 minutes, adding small amounts of water as needed to prevent sticking.
3. Reduce heat, cover, and steam until tender, about 15 minutes. Serve hot or cold.

Insights: Artichokes are thistle flowers, which, in time, will open up and expose their beauty. For culinary purposes, however, choose young, firm artichokes with their leaves tightly closed. Store them whole in a sealed container or plastic bag in the refrigerator to keep them from drying out. They can be steamed, boiled, or baked, whole or with the leaves removed, and the delicate inner heart can be sautéed or eaten raw. Artichokes contain a "choke," which must be carefully removed with a spoon before eating. Simply scoop it out and discard it.

French Oven-Roasted Garlic

serves 4

4 whole heads fresh garlic (choose firm garlic clusters
with large cloves)

1. Preheat oven to 300 degrees.
2. Remove the excess layers of papery skin from the outside
   of each head of garlic, without disturbing the last layer,
   which holds the cloves together.
3. Place the garlic heads in a baking dish and bake, covered,
   for 1 hour.
4. Remove cover and continue baking until garlic begins to
   smell fragrant and ooze out of the top.
5. Allow the roasted garlic to cool slightly, then slice the top
   off of each head so that the sweet soft flesh of the garlic
   can be scooped out with a knife or squeezed out.
6. Either squeeze out the garlic paste to serve as a spread or
   place whole heads of roasted garlic on individual plates
   for guests to scoop out themselves. Serve with toasted
   baquettes, *Multi-Grain Essene Bread,* or *Sprouted Grain
   Crisps* (see pg. 138, 143).

Insights: Elephant garlic has the largest cloves and the
mildest flavor. Its natural sweetness and large cloves lend
themselves well to roasting. Garlic varies in strength, so
the amount you use in a recipe can vary. A good rule is to
use less and add more after tasting.

Sweet, smooth, and luscious
is the final result of roasting
garlic. Use it alone, as a fat-
free paté, or added to more sinful
spreads—it's unbelievably good!

*Guardian Angel,
please help me
develop grace,
humor and wisdom,
so that I may be
more like You.*

Clean white mushrooms are so pretty when they're served like this—simple and wonderful, with pinenuts and a hint of minty basil. (See *Insights* below.)

*Guardian Angel,
please help me see my
true path in life and
be courageous enough
to take it.*

Stuffed Raw Mushrooms

serves 4

12 jumbo mushrooms, wiped clean
1 clove fresh garlic, crushed
1/2 cup pine nuts, soaked for 6–8 hours and minced
1/4 cup parsley, washed, dried, and minced
1 tsp. minced fresh basil
2 tsp. light miso

1. Using a small spoon, carefully scoop out center of mushrooms, leaving about 1/4 inch of flesh around the perimeter. Save stems and centers to use later. (Good for soup, broth base, or gravy.) Set mushroom shells aside.
2. Combine remaining ingredients and stir well.
3. Pack mushroom shells with filling and serve slightly warmed in the oven (at lowest temperature setting) or at room temperature.

Insights: Basil is a member of the mint family and is revered for its fragrant leaves. It's used extensively in Italy, and Thailand as well as other countries. Its broad, shiny leaves, ranging in color from green to purple, exude an unmistakable aroma that is excellent in salads, dressings, pasta sauces, and spreads. Save the stems to add to fresh vegetable juices and broths.

French Walnut Mushrooms

serves 4

olive oil cooking spray or 1/2 tsp. olive oil
1 Tbsp. shallots, minced
2 cloves garlic, crushed
8 jumbo mushrooms, washed and dried
1/2 cup walnuts, slightly toasted and ground
1 Tbsp. minced parsley
1/2 Tbsp. vegan egg replacer in 2 Tbsp. water

1. Heat non-stick skillet to medium and season with oil. Sauté shallots and garlic gently until soft, about 3 to 4 minutes, adding small amounts of water as needed to prevent sticking.
2. Meanwhile, scoop out stems and some pulp from each of the mushrooms.
3. Combine all ingredients, except mushrooms, and mix thoroughly.
4. Spoon a little of the mixture into each mushroom cavity, forming a small mound on top.
5. Bake, covered, in a preheated 350 degree oven for 30 minutes. Remove the cover and bake another 10 minutes. Serve hot or at room temperature.

This appetizer is a gourmet delight with its toasted walnuts and garlicky aroma. It's the kind of dish that the French delight in, which can also be served as an outstanding accompaniment to a main course.

Guardian Angel,
please help me
appreciate life
and the blessings
in all things.

Naturally low in fat and high in protein, these "nuts" make a great snack for your guests while you're putting dinner together. Also, keep them on hand for the "little angels" when they come home from school.

Guardian Angel, please help me graciously accept assistance from the Celestial Realms.

Middle Eastern Seasoned Garbanzo Nuts
makes 2 cups

1 3/4 dry cups garbanzos (chickpeas), soak overnight, sprout 2 days (for sprouting information see pg. 9)
2 Tbsp. unpasteurized light miso
1 tsp. onion powder
1 tsp. ground coriander
1 tsp. ground cumin
1/2 tsp. garlic powder
1/8 tsp. cayenne pepper

1. Dry sprouts on a towel to remove excess moisture.
2. Combine remaining ingredients and toss with garbanzos.
3. Place beans on a dehydrator sheet, allowing some space in between each bean, and dehydrate 8 to 12 hours.
4. Serve warm for snacks or keep stored in refrigerator.

Spicy Sprouted Lentil Nuts
makes 2 cups

1 3/4 dry cups lentils, soak overnight, sprout 1 1/2 days (for sprouting information see pg. 9)
1 Tbsp. each soy sauce and Braggs Liquid Aminos®
1/2 Tbsp. mild curry powder
1 tsp. Onion Magic® or onion powder
1/8 tsp. each garlic powder and cayenne pepper

1. Dry sprouts on a clean towel to remove excess moisture.
2. Combine remaining ingredients and toss with lentil sprouts.
3. Place lentils on dehydrator sheets, allowing some space in between each lentil, and dehydrate 8 to 12 hours.
4. Serve warm or keep stored in refrigerator.

Seasoned Sunflower Seeds

makes 2 cups

2 cups dry raw shelled sunflower seeds, soak overnight,
   sprout 1 day (For sprouting information see pg. 8)
2 Tbsp. tamari soy sauce
1 tsp. Onion Magic® or onion powder
1/8 tsp. garlic powder
1/8 tsp. cayenne pepper

1. Dry sunflower sprouts on a clean towel. Place in a bowl and
   toss with remaining ingredients.
2. Spread seeds on dehydrator sheets, allowing space between
   them, and dehydrate 8 to 12 hours.
3. Store in refrigerator.

Tamari Almonds

makes 2 cups

2 cups dry whole raw almonds, soak 24 hours
2 Tbsp. tamari soy sauce
1/4 tsp. onion powder
1/8 tsp. garlic powder
1/8 tsp. natural hickory smoke seasoning

1 Dry soaked, drained almonds on a clean towel.
2. Combine remaining ingredients in a bowl, add almonds, and
   toss well.
3. Place on dehydrator sheets, allowing space between each
   one to facilitate drying, and dehydrate 24 hours.
4. Store in refrigerator.

These little powerhouses of energy are as delicious as they are nutritious! Because they are sprouted and uncooked, they are lower in fat and easily digested. Eat them as a snack or sprinkle them over salads.

*Guardian Angel,
please guide me with
benevolence
through my lessons.*

Don't expect this to taste anything like fish eggs! It has a delicately delicious, slightly smoky taste and a caviar-like texture.

Guardian Angel, please help me remember to add the most important ingredient of all, Love.

Eggplant Caviar

serves 4

1 large eggplant
olive oil cooking spray
1 clove garlic, crushed
1/2 tsp. organic lemon peel, finely grated
1/4 tsp. sea salt (or, to taste)
1/8 tsp. white pepper

Sprouted Grain Crisps (see pg. 143)
1/2 cup *Tofu "Egg" Salad* (see following recipe)
1/2 cup red onions, minced

1. Slice eggplant in half lengthwise and spray oil on cut side. Place in 400 degree oven for 45 minutes or until inside is soft and skin is charred.
2. Scoop out inside of eggplant and mash thoroughly. Mix with garlic, lemon peel, salt, and pepper.
3. Chill and serve as a spread on toast or *Sprouted Grain Crisps* with *Tofu "Egg" Salad* and minced onions on the side.

Tofu "Egg" Salad

makes 1/2 cup

olive oil cooking spray or 1/2 tsp. olive oil
1 Tbsp. shallots, minced
2 ounces firm tofu
1/8 tsp. turmeric
1 Tbsp. fresh chives, thinly sliced
1/8 tsp. sea salt (or, to taste)

1. Heat small non-stick skillet to medium and season with oil. Gently cook shallots until tender, about 3 to 4 minutes, adding small amounts of water as needed to prevent sticking. Add the turmeric and cook another minute.
2. Using a fork, crush the tofu so that it resembles egg salad.
3. Toss all ingredients together so that some of the tofu is still a little white and retains a cooked "egg white" appearance.

Insights: Chives are the mildest member of the onion family. They have tubular leaves and beautiful, edible purple flowers, which can be added to cooked foods toward the end of cooking time or used as a garnish. Chives are easily grown indoors in flower pots. The seeds also make wonderful sprouts for sandwiches and salads.

This looks and tastes very similar to egg salad and is a great accompaniment to *Eggplant Caviar.* (See opposite page.) Serve it as you would any egg salad—on crackers, as a dip for veggies, or in sandwiches.

Guardian Angel, please help me be more generous with my love and understanding.

Smooth and rich, these nut butters are easy to make and require no additional oil. When you make them yourself you can be assured that they are fresh and far more digestible than roasted nut butters.

Guardian Angel,
please help me
let go of the past
and forgive,
so that I may love.

Cashew Butter

makes 1 1/2 cups

1 pound raw cashews

1. Put cashews in a food processor. Using the "S" blade, grind until smooth and sticky. (If using a Champion Juicer® , use the blank filter and homogenize cashews as directed.)
2. Stored in an airtight container in the refrigerator, it will keep for up to one month.

Sweet Almond Spread

makes 2 cups

2 cups raw almonds
2 Tbsp. Sucanat® (dehydrated sugar cane juice)
purified water

1. Put almonds in a food processor. Using the "S" blade, or a nut grinder, grind to a fine powder.
2. Add Sucanat® and pulse to mix. (If using a nut grinder, mix by hand.)
3. Add water in small amounts, pulsing, until a thick spread has formed. (If using a nut grinder, mix by hand.)
4. Serve as a spread with *Multi-Grain Essene Bread* (see pg. 138), *Date Walnut Scones* (see pg. 142), or fruit leathers (see pg. 46, 47).
5. Stored in an airtight container in the refrigerator, it will keep for up to two weeks.

Artichoke Paté

makes 1 1/2 cups

4 whole fresh artichokes
1 cup *Almond* or *Cashew Cheese* (see pg. 22, 23)
1 Tbsp. nutritional yeast
1/2 tsp. Vege-Sal® or sea salt
1 tsp. ground basil or 1 Tbsp. fresh minced basil
1 small clove garlic, crushed
pinch of ground nutmeg and white pepper

1. Remove the leaves from artichokes and save for later use.
2. Scoop out the tough, fibrous "choke" and discard.
3. Chop the remaining portion of the artichoke (the "heart") and place in blender. Add remaining ingredients and purée.
4. Serve with raw vegetables and *Sprouted Grain Crisps* (see pg. 143). Can be stored in refrigerator for up to 4 days.

Herb Cheese Spread

makes 1 1/2 cups

3/4 cup *Almond* or *Cashew Cheese* (see pg. 22, 23)
1/4 cup pine nuts, chopped
1/4 cup red onion, minced
1 green onion, minced
1 Tbsp. light miso
1/2 Tbsp. nutritional yeast
1 clove garlic, crushed
2 Tbsp. parsley, minced
1 tsp. dill weed
freshly ground pepper to taste

1. Combine ingredients and stir well.
2. Serve with *Sprouted Grain Crisps* (see pg. 143), or use as a dip for raw vegetables.

Raw artichoke hearts with basil and garlic make this paté one of my favorites! This herb cheese spread, which is chunky and has a hint of dill, is great as a filling for mushrooms, celery, or cherry tomatoes. If you wish, you may substitute whipped tofu for nut cheese.

Guardian Angel,
please help me
become a great
inspiration to others.

This recipe was inspired by a recipe I found years ago in *Sunset* magazine that called for using (dairy) cream cheese. I first revised the recipe using tofu, and later created a raw version, which has become my personal favorite. It is gorgeous and incredibly delicious!

Guardian Angel,
please help me
give up distractions,
which keep me from
developing spiritually.

Italian Pesto Almond Torte

serves 8–12

Pesto:
1 cup tightly packed fresh basil leaves, washed and dried
2 tsp. flax oil or extra-virgin olive oil
1 Tbsp. water
2 Tbsp. raw pine nuts or walnuts
1 small clove garlic, crushed
1/4 tsp. sea salt

2 cups *Seasoned Almond Cheese* or *Almond Ricotta* (see pg. 26, 28)

1 leaf fresh basil

Sprouted Grain Crisps (see pg. 143)
raw vegetable platter

1. Place *Pesto* ingredients in a blender or food processor, and pulverize until smooth. (Remove cover and scrape sides with a spatula several times to insure consistency.)
2. Line a 4- or 5-inch colander or a clean (new), vented flower pot with a double layer of damp cheesecloth, draping the excess over the rim of the top.

3. Spoon 1/4 of the cheese into the bottom of the pot, and press the mixture down firmly and evenly with the back of a spoon.

4. Using a different spoon, spread 1/3 of the *Pesto* evenly on top of the cheese and press it down firmly and evenly.

5. Continue layering, using 1/3 of the remaining cheese on top of the *Pesto*, then 1/2 of the remaining *Pesto,* and 1/2 of the remaining cheese, then the rest of the *Pesto*, and finish with the rest of the cheese. Press each layer down in turn until layering is complete.

6. Fold excess cheesecloth smoothly over the cheese, and place colander in a bowl with a weight on top of the cheesecloth. Cover the container with plastic wrap and place in the refrigerator for 2 to 3 hours or overnight. (Expect some whey to drain from the cheese.)

7. To serve, fold back cheesecloth and invert the torte onto a serving plate. Gently peel off cheesecloth and garnish the top with a single basil leaf.

8. Serve as a spread with *Sprouted Grain Crisps* and raw vegetables.

When basil is in season, make large batches of pesto and freeze them in ice cube trays. When frozen, transfer them to an airtight container and store in freezer to use as needed.

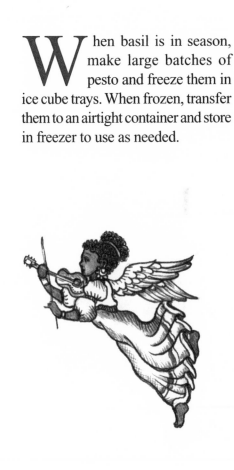

Guardian Angel, please help me know that to serve others is to give and receive blessings.

A classic favorite at every party, this non-dairy dip is even better than the original! It also makes a great filling for mushrooms, celery, and cherry tomatoes.

Guardian Angel,
please help me
cultivate an awareness
of the Divine
in all things.

French Onion Dip

makes 2–3 cups

2 cups *Almond* or *Cashew Cheese* (see pg. 22, 23)
1 Tbsp. dark miso paste
1 1/2 tsp. garlic powder
1 tsp. tamari soy sauce
2 tsp. onion powder
1 tsp. Sucanat® (dehydrated sugar cane juice)
3 Tbsp. toasted dehydrated onions
1 cup purified water (or, as needed)

1. Combine ingredients together, adding enough water to achieve desired consistency.
2. Serve as a spread for *Savory Sunflower Bread Stix* (see pg. 140), or *Sprouted Grain Crisps* (see pg. 143), or as a dip for fresh vegetables.
3. Can be stored in refrigerator for up to one week.

Note: Dip will thicken as it sits. More water may be needed after storing it in the refrigerator.

Roasted Garlic Cheese Spread

makes 1 1/4 cup

2 whole heads fresh garlic (choose heads with large firm
   cloves tightly clustered)
1 cup *Almond* or *Cashew Cheese* (see pg. 22, 23)
1 Tbsp. nutritional yeast
2 tsp. light miso paste
pinch of ground nutmeg
pinch of white pepper

1. Preheat oven to 350 degrees.
2. Wrap whole heads of unpeeled garlic in foil and bake for 1
   hour, or until the flesh of the garlic is tender and soft.
3. Remove the flesh from the skin and mash well. Discard skin.
4. Combine garlic with remaining ingredients and mix well.
5. Serve as a spread for *Multi-Grain Essene Bread* (see pg.
   138)*, Fragrant Onion Herb Rolls* (see pg. 144), or *Sprouted
   Grain Crisps* (see pg. 143), or as a dip for fresh vegetables.
6. Can be stored in refrigerator for up to one week.

Insights: Nutritional yeast, not to be confused with brewers yeast or active (baking) yeast, is available in powder or flake form. It's high in protein and minerals, and some brands, such as Red Star®, also contain vitamin B$_{12}$, an essential nutrient that can be illusive in a pure vegetarian diet. It has a cheese-like flavor and is delicious added to sauces, gravies, and spreads.

Roasted garlic is the secret ingredient in this sinfully delicious spread. It's also wonderful mixed with mashed potatoes, or, with the addition of lemon juice and a little water, to use over salads and other raw food dishes. Yum!

*Guardian Angel,
please help me
not be judgmental
of myself and others.*

This tangy sesame spread is actually a thicker version of the sauce that is used over Middle Eastern falafels.

Pungent and garlicky, this Southeast Asian-inspired peanut dip is also great as a filling for mushrooms, celery, or cherry tomatoes.

*Guardian Angel,
please help me
let go of negative
thoughtforms, which
keep me from
my highest growth.*

Middle Eastern Sesame Spread

serves 4

6 Tbsp. raw tahini (sesame seed butter)
1–2 cloves of garlic, crushed
1/4 cup lemon juice
1/4 tsp. sea salt (or, to taste)
3 Tbsp. water (or just enough to achieve a thick dip or spread)

1. Combine first 4 ingredients and mix well.
2. Slowly add water, blending thoroughly.
3. Serve at room temperature as a spread for *Sprouted Grain Crisps* or *Sprouted Rye Essene Rolls* (see pg. 143, 139), or as a dip for fresh vegetables. Will keep in refrigerator for up to one week.

Indonesian Peanut Dip

makes 1 cup

1/2 cup smooth peanut butter
1/4 cup onion, minced
1/4 cup fresh lime juice
1 Tbsp. tamari soy sauce
1 tsp. garlic, crushed
1 tsp. ground coriander
1/4 cup parsley, minced

1. Hand mix ingredients together thoroughly.
2. Serve at room temperature as a spread for *Sea Vegetable Grain Crisps* (see pg. 143) or *Multi-Grain Essene Bread* (see pg. 138), or as a dip for fresh vegetables. Will keep in refrigerator for up to one week.

Mediterranean Green Olive & Pesto Tapenade

serves 4

10–12 large green olives, pitted
1/4 cup *Pesto,* (see pg. 70)
1/2 red onion, chopped
1 Tbsp. flax oil or extra-virgin olive oil
1/2 tsp. thyme

1. Combine ingredients in a food processor and pulse mix, removing lid several times to scrape sides with a spatula. Mixture should be smooth, but not totally puréed.
2. Serve with *Sprouted Grain Crisps* (see pg. 143).

Mediterranean Black Olive & Walnut Tapenade

makes 1 cup

1 cup black niçoise or Greek olives, pitted
1/2 cup walnuts, ground
1 clove garlic, crushed
3 Tbsp. capers
1 Tbsp. flax oil or extra-virgin olive oil
2 tsp. lemon juice
1/2 tsp. crushed oregano
1/4 tsp. ground thyme
1/4 tsp. ground basil

1. Combine ingredients in a food processor and pulse mix, removing lid several times to scrape sides with a spatula. Mixture should be smooth, but not totally puréed.
2. Serve on *Sprouted Grain Crisps* (see pg. 143).

O lives are a staple and abundant food of the Mediterranean and have been enjoyed there for centuries. I like both green and black olive varieties of tapenade with different seasonings. Here are my two favorite recipes—Buon Appetito!

*Guardian Angel,
please help me
always see
the Light of God
in myself and others.*

I'm told that my first solid food as a baby, was avocado. I'm sure I cooed, "Mmm" when I tasted it then, because I still do! I keep my *Guacamole* simple, so as not to overpower the delicate flavor of the avocado. Mmmmm.

Guardian Angel, please help me pay attention, so that all my lessons are benevolent.

Guacamole
(Mexican Avocado Dip)

serves 4

2 medium avocados, cut in half, peeled, and seeded
1/4 cup onion, minced
1 clove garlic, crushed
1 Tbsp. lemon juice
1/8 tsp. cayenne pepper (or, to taste)
1/4 tsp. sea salt (or, to taste)

1. Mash avocado with a fork until almost smooth.
2. Combine remaining ingredients and hand mix thoroughly.
3. Serve as a spread for *Sprouted Grain Crisps* or *Savory Sprouted Sunflower Bread Stiks* (see pg. 143, 140), or as a dip for fresh vegetables. Must be used immediately or avocado will turn brown and change flavor.

Insights: Choose firm avocados and allow them to ripen at home where they won't be molested by curious shoppers. When they begin to give to gentle pressure, place them in the refrigerator until you need them. To store partially used avocados, leave the seed in and squeeze lemon juice or *Rejuvilac* (see pg. 15) over the cut side. Wrap tightly in plastic wrap and store in the refrigerator.

Baba Ghanouj (Middle Eastern Eggplant Sesame Dip)

serves 6

1 large eggplant, roasted under broiler, skinned, and
    chopped (See *Insights*, below.)
1 tsp. sea salt (or, to taste)
3 Tbsp. raw tahini (sesame seed butter)
2 Tbsp. lemon juice
dash of cayenne pepper
2 medium cloves garlic, crushed

1. Combine ingredients together in food processor or blender
   and pureé until smooth.
2. Serve at room temperature with *Savory Sunflower Bread Stix*
   (see pg. 140), or *Sprouted Grain Crisps* (see pg. 143), or as
   a dip for fresh vegetables.

Insights: Choose an eggplant that is smooth, firm, and
blemish free. To roast an eggplant, slice it in half lengthwise and spray the cut side with a little oil. Place in a preheated 400 degree oven and bake for 40 to 45 minutes, or
until the skin is charred and the flesh is soft. Peel the skin
off and discard. The flesh, which is naturally sweet and delicious, may be chopped or puréed.

Even if you think you don't like eggplant, this combina-tion of eggplant, sesame and garlic, creates a whole new flavor that you will love in this heavenly spread.

*Guardian Angel,
please help me
remember to call upon
entities of
Light and Love.*

Sprouted garbanzos, or chick peas as they are also called, are used to make this uncooked version of the *Traditional Lebanese Garbanzo & Sesame Dip*. (See opposite page.) It's wonderful with a crisp raw vegetable platter or *Sprouted Grain Crisps*. (See pg. 143.)

Guardian Angel, please help me walk through life in safety and harmony.

New Age Hummus
(Sprouted Garbanzo & Sesame Dip)

serves 6

1 cup sprouted garbanzo beans
   (for sprouting information see pg. 9)
1 Tbsp. light miso (or, to taste)
1/2 cup raw tahini (sesame seed butter)
1 Tbsp. lemon juice
1 tsp. ground cumin
1/2 tsp. paprika
dash of cayenne pepper
1–2 cloves garlic, crushed
2–4 Tbsp. water (as needed)

1. Purée mixture together in a food processor or blender, slowly adding water, until thick and creamy.
2. Serve at room temperature with pita bread, raw vegetables, or *Sprouted Grain Crisps* (see pg. 143).

Insights: Garbanzo beans sprout in 2 to 3 days, but require a little more love than other sprouts. I recommend rinsing them 3 times a day instead of 2, and talking to them—they like that!

Hummus
(Traditional Lebanese Garbanzo & Sesame Dip)

serves 6

16 ounces cooked garbanzo beans, drained
1/2 tsp. sea salt (or, to taste)
3 Tbsp. raw tahini (sesame seed butter)
2 Tbsp. lemon juice
1/2 tsp. ground cumin
1/4 tsp. paprika
dash of cayenne pepper
1–2 cloves garlic, crushed
2–4 Tbsp. purified water (as needed)

1. Purée ingredients together in food processor or blender, slowly adding water as needed, until thick and creamy.
2. Serve at room temperature as a spread for pita bread or *Sprouted Grain Crisps* (see pg. 143), or as a dip for fresh vegetables.

Insights: To cook garbanzo beans, also known as chick peas, soak them overnight (1 cup beans to 3 cups water), then rinse and drain in the morning. Cover with purified water and bring to a boil. Reduce heat to simmer, with lid slightly ajar to allow steam to vent, and cook for 2 to 3 hours, or until tender. The broth is great for soups and tastes a little like chicken broth, hence the name, chick peas.

Good and garlicky, this Middle Eastern favorite is delicious served with *Falafels, Sprouted Grain Crisps,* and *Horiatiki Salad.* (See pg. 179, 143, 84.)

*Guardian Angel,
please help me know
that life is easy
if I simply
allow it to be so.*

Chapter Six

Sacred Salads

A Talk with Spirit about Releasing the Past

Divine Guardian, please assist me in letting go of that which no longer serves my highest good. Help me learn from the past and let go of it, so I may focus my attention on the present. I wish to be mindful of the moment, knowing that in this sacred moment everything is divinely inspired. My intention is to become consciously aware of the perfect now and to feel the energy of Universal Life Force flowing through me. I ask for assistance in releasing all blocks and limitations that impede my mental, emotional, physical and spiritual well-being.

I ask that the food I'm preparing be life affirming and provide me with all my nutritional needs. I know this is a gift of Divine love and blessings, and I acknowledge it. I love you, I bless you, I am one with you and All That Is.

Recipes at a Glance

Sacred Salads

Peppers, avocados, tomatoes, and corn are staples throughout Mexico and unite together to form this colorful, tasty salad. If you like spicy food, add a minced jalapeno or a couple of minced, serrano chiles. Spicy or mild, it's delicious!

Guardian Angel, please illuminate the path of Light for me.

Mexican Corn & Avocado Salad

serves 4–6

2 fresh Anaheim peppers (long green chilies)
2 ears corn (about 2 cups), kernels removed from cob
2 green onions, thinly sliced
1/2 sweet red pepper, diced
1/4 cup cilantro (Chinese parsley), chopped
1 Tbsp. flax oil or extra-virgin olive oil
2 cups small cherry tomatoes
2 Tbsp. lime juice
1 small clove garlic, crushed
1/2 tsp. sea salt or Braggs Liquid Amino® to taste
1 medium avocado
1/2 cup sprouted pumpkin seeds (see pg. 8)

1. Arrange chilies on a baking sheet and roast under oven broiler, turning, until skin is scorched and blistered.
2. Gently remove skins from chilies, being careful not to break them.
3. Cut the chilies in half lengthwise, and remove the stems and seeds. Slice chilies crosswise, 1/4-inch thick. (If canned chilies are used, rinse, drain, remove seeds, and slice crosswise.)
4. Combine all ingredients, except avocado, and toss well.
5. Peel avocado and cut into 1/2-inch cubes and gently fold into salad mixture.
6. Top with pumpkin seeds, and serve as soon as possible.

Mexican Fiesta Salad

serves 4–6

Fiesta Dressing:
1 Tbsp. fresh lemon or lime juice
1 Tbsp. flax oil or extra-virgin olive oil
1/2 tsp. ground cumin
1/4 tsp. ground coriander
1/8 tsp. cayenne pepper
sea salt and pepper to taste

2 ears corn (2 cups kernels), kernels removed from cob
1 cup sprouted lentils or sprouted azuki beans (see pg. 9)
1 cup jicama, peeled and diced
1 Anaheim pepper (long green chili), sliced crosswise
1/2 red bell pepper, diced
12 pitted black olives, sliced or quartered
1/4 cup small red onion, julienned
4–6 radishes, thinly sliced
1/4 cup fresh cilantro (Chinese parsley), minced
1/4 cup fresh parsley, minced
1/2 head romaine lettuce, washed and broken into pieces
1/2 firm avocado, peeled, seeded, and diced

1. Combine all ingredients for dressing and stir well.
2. Add remaining ingredients and toss. Serve immediately.

Celebrate life with fresh corn from the garden united with crisp and juicy jicama and cilantro. I've taken the liberty of replacing cooked beans with living bean sprouts, but you may prefer to use cooked black beans or pintos. It's great both ways!

*Guardian Angel,
please help me see
the evidence of
your guidance
in my life.*

Horiatiki is one of my all-time favorite salads. I have replaced the usual sheep's feta with *Almond Feta-ish Cheese,* (see pg. 29) and it is heavenly! For a satisfying lunch or light supper, serve it with *Sprouted Grain Crisps* and *Baba Ganouj.* (See pg. 143, 77.)

Guardian Angel,
please help me
allow love to unfold
in my life.

Horiatiki
(Greek Salad with Almond Feta)

serves 4

Greek Salad Dressing:
1 Tbsp. flax oil or extra-virgin olive oil
2 Tbsp. water
1 Tbsp. lemon juice
1 tsp. whole dried oregano
1/2 tsp. sea salt (or, to taste)
freshly ground pepper to taste

Salad:
4 medium tomatoes, cut into large chunks
1 cucumber, cut in half lengthwise,
   seeded, and sliced crosswise
1 large green bell pepper, cut into quarters and sliced
1 small red onion, sliced thin
1/2 head romaine lettuce, washed and broken into pieces
24 Greek olives
1/2 cup *Feta-ish Almond Cheese* (see pg. 29)
   - cut into 1/2-inch cubes

1. Combine ingredients for *Dressing* and set aside.
2. Combine ingredients for *Salad,* except for cheese; add dressing and toss well.
3. Serve *Horiatiki* on individual plates and top with *Feta-ish Cheese.* Serve immediately.

Salad Niçoise
(French Garden Salad)

serves 4

Vinaigrette:
juice of 1 lime
1 Tbsp. flax oil or extra-virgin olive oil
3 Tbsp. water
1/2 clove garlic, crushed
1 tsp. shallots, minced
1 tsp. dijon-style prepared mustard
1/4 tsp. Colemans® dry mustard
1/4 tsp. sea salt (or, to taste)
freshly ground pepper

Salad:
1 head bibb or green-leaf lettuce, washed and dried
2 red potatoes, boiled and sliced into 1/4-inch rounds
24 fresh green beans, boiled for 3 to 4 minutes, then rinsed in ice water
16 fresh asparagus, boiled for 3 to 4 minutes, then rinsed in ice water
2 small ripe tomatoes, quartered
4 mushrooms, washed, dried, and sliced paper thin
1/2 cucumber, sliced
4–6 ounces smoked or baked seasoned tofu, julienned
12 niçoise or Greek olives
1 Tbsp. capers

1. Mix ingredients for *Vinaigrette* and set aside.
2. Prepare each salad individually, laying down a flat bed of lettuce and attractively grouping each vegetable on top.
3. Sprinkle the capers over the potatoes, and gently pour some dressing over each salad just prior to serving. Serve at room temperature.

This traditional French salad is a feast for the eyes as well as the palate! I have replaced the conventional tuna with tofu in this recipe, though I have also used avocado as a substitute. We enjoy it as a full meal at lunch or dinner with *Sprouted Grain Crisps* and *Olive Tapinade*. (See pg. 143, 75.)

*Guardian Angel,
please strengthen me
and give me the courage
to follow my dreams.*

Young sunflower greens and living bean sprouts make this delicious salad a true vitality builder! You can also vary it by using baby lettuces or spinach in place of sunflower greens. We never tire of the many variations of this recipe for good health.

Guardian Angel,
please stimulate an
awareness of the
presence of angels
in my life.

California Sunshine Salad

serves 4

California Sunshine Dressing:
2 Tbsp. red onion, minced
2 Tbsp. Braggs Liquid Aminos® (or, to taste)
1 Tbsp. flax oil or extra-virgin olive oil
1/2 tsp. Onion Magic® seasoning
freshly ground pepper

4 cups sunflower greens, chopped (see pg. 11)
2 large tomatoes, chopped
1 cup mixed bean sprouts, (see pg. 9)
1/2 avocado, peeled and diced
1/2 medium zucchini, julienned
1/2 yellow squash, julienned

1. Mix *Dressing* ingredients together and set aside.
2. Combine all ingredients together with dressing and toss well. Serve immediately.

Sunomono
(Japanese Pickled Cucumber Salad)

serves 4

2 medium cucumbers, peeled,
   cut in half lengthwise, and seeded
2 tsp. salt in 2 cups water
3 Tbsp. rice vinegar
1/4 cup purified water
1 Tbsp. brown rice syrup
1/2 tsp. Tamari soy sauce
1/2 tsp. sea salt

1 tsp. toasted sesame seeds

1. Slice cucumbers crosswise as thin as possible, forming crescent shapes. Soak in salted water for 1 hour, drain, and squeeze out excess liquid using your hands.
2. Combine remaining ingredients, except sesame seeds, and mix until syrup is dissolved.
3. Marinate cucumbers in mixture for a couple of hours in refrigerator.
4. Drain liquid; separate cucumbers into small individual serving dishes, and garnish with sesame seeds. Serve chilled.

Sweet and pungent, this traditional Japanese salad is easy to prepare and delightfully refreshing! We enjoy it with *Japanese Sushimaki* or with *Hawaiian Teriyaki Tempeh Brochettes*. (See pg. 166, 181.)

Guardian Angel,
please help me
know that I am
one with all
of God's creations.

The lightly toasted walnuts add texture and a nutty flavor that make this dish really special! Cabbage is one of the most versatile of all vegetables. It can be eaten raw, cultured, cooked, or as in this recipe, merely wilted.

Guardian Angel, please help me discover the angelic world of Love, Joy, and Blessings.

Austrian Wilted Cabbage & Walnut Salad

serves 4

Dressing:
1/2 Tbsp. lime juice or wine vinegar
1 Tbsp. flax oil or walnut oil
1 Tbsp. water
1/2 clove garlic, crushed
1 tsp. shallots, minced
1 tsp. dijon-style prepared mustard
1/8 tsp. powdered dry mustard (Colemans®)
1/4 tsp. sea salt
freshly ground pepper

olive oil cooking spray or 1/2 tsp. olive oil
1 large onion, julienned
2 cloves garlic, minced
1 head cabbage, shredded
1/2 cup walnuts, lightly toasted and coarsely chopped
paprika

1. Combine ingredients for dressing and set aside.
2. Heat non-stick skillet to medium and season with oil. Sauté onion and garlic until transparent, about 5 minutes, adding small amounts of water, as needed, to prevent sticking.
3. Add cabbage to skillet, reduce heat to medium-low, and cover. Cook, turning as needed, until cabbage is completely wilted.
4. Toss cabbage, walnuts, and dressing together, and allow to cool prior to serving. Garnish with paprika.

Minnesota Coleslaw

serves 4

Dressing:
2 Tbsp. *Garlic Vegannaise* (see below)
2 Tbsp. water
1/4 tsp. onion powder
1/4 tsp. paprika
1/4 tsp. powdered dry mustard (Colemans®)

1 1/2 cups cabbage, finely shredded
1 cup carrots, finely shredded
1 Tbsp. minced parsley

1. Combine ingredients for dressing and mix well.
2. Toss dressing with vegetables and chill for at least one hour prior to serving.

Garlic Vegannaise

makes 1 pint

10 1/2 ounces (1 carton) soft silken tofu
2 Tbsp. tahini (sesame seed butter)
1/4 cup lemon juice
1 clove garlic, crushed
1 Tbsp. brown rice syrup
1 tsp. nutritional yeast
1 tsp. dijon-style mustard
1 tsp. sea salt

1. Combine ingredients in a blender and purée until smooth, using as much water as needed to achieve desired consistency.

When I was growing up I thought coleslaw was pronounced "cold" slaw, probably because it was always chilled. We like this simple version made with this *Garlic Vegannaise* and colorful, shredded carrots.

Guardian Angel, please help me remember my Divine origins.

We never tire of beautiful red, ripe, organically grown tomatoes! If you are still buying the anemic non-organic variety, do yourself a favor and make a trip to the nearest organic produce market—it's well worth it!

Guardian Angel, please help me experience life's simple joys.

Mediterranean Tomato Salad

serves 4–6

2 heads endive or arugula lettuce
4–6 ripe tomatoes, peeled and thinly sliced
1 Tbsp. minced parsley
1 Tbsp. minced chives
1 Tbsp. minced fresh basil
1 Tbsp. flax oil or extra-virgin olive oil
1 Tbsp. lime juice or balsamic vinegar
2 Tbsp. purified water
sea salt and freshly ground pepper to taste

1. Attractively arrange lettuce around the edge of a serving dish.
2. Place the tomatoes on top and sprinkle with herbs.
3. Mix together the lime juice, oil, and water, and pour evenly over the top.
4. Salt and pepper to taste and serve at once.

Insight: Choose tomatoes that are smooth and red without high hips. Never store tomatoes in the refrigerator or they will change texture and become mushy. Instead, keep them in a light area of the kitchen, out of the hot sunlight. They will continue to ripen and increase in sweetness.

Stuffed Tomatoes

serves 4

4 large tomatoes
1 medium-size ripe avocado, peeled, seeded, and mashed
1 Tbsp. lime or lemon juice
1/2 tsp. sea salt (or, to taste)
1/4 cup fresh young peas or sprouted peas (see pg. 9)
1/2 cup leeks, thinly sliced crosswise
1 stalk celery, thinly sliced
2 small radishes, thinly sliced
1/2 green bell pepper, seeded and diced
onion or radish sprouts (see pg. 8)

1. Carefully scoop out the center of the tomato, leaving 1/4- to 1/2-inch of flesh around the outside. Set aside the hollowed-out tomato shells and dice the rest.
2. Combine avocado, lime, and salt, and mix well.
3. Add remaining ingredients, including diced tomatoes but excluding onion or radish sprouts, and stir gently.
4. Scoop the vegetable filling into the tomato shells, piling the filling high. Garnish with sprouts, and serve chilled or at room temperature.

All dressed up naturally, these stuffed tomatoes tell your guests how special they are! They are beautiful, unique and perfect!

*Guardian Angel,
please help me know
that I am a part of
the perfection
of nature.*

I was inspired to create this savory recipe after tasting one similar at a Thai restaurant in Santa Rosa, California. They roasted their eggplant, and you may prefer to do that, but I find it easier to prepare and just as delicious uncooked.

Guardian Angel, please help me live my life fully and peacefully.

California Thai Salad

serves 4

Spicy Thai Dressing:
juice of 1 lime
1 Tbsp. fresh hot red chilies (or, to taste), seeded and finely minced
1 Tbsp. fresh lemongrass (or 1/2 tsp. organically grown lemon peel), minced
1/2 clove garlic, crushed
1/2 tsp. sea salt (or, to taste)
1/2 tsp. pure maple syrup

1 cup Japanese eggplant, peeled and cut into small cubes
1 cup jicama (or fresh water chestnuts), peeled and cut into small cubes
12 small cherry tomatoes, cut into halves
1/2 small head radicchio lettuce, broken into pieces
1/2 firm papaya, peeled, seeded, and cut into small cubes
1/2 medium-size Asian pear (or any firm pear), cored and cut into small cubes
1/4 cup red onion, sliced paper thin, then quartered
1 small green onion, sliced thin
6 mint leaves, cut into fine shreds
2 large leaves fresh basil, cut into fine shreds
1/4 cup pomegranate seeds

1. Prepare dressing and set aside.
2. Combine remaining ingredients and toss gently.
3. Pour dressing over top and toss gently once again.
4. Serve chilled or at room temperature.

Thai Spinach Salad in Peanut Coconut Sauce

serves 4

Peanut Coconut Sauce:
olive oil cooking spray or 1/2 tsp. toasted sesame oil
2 cloves garlic, minced
1/4 tsp. ground fresh chili paste
1 Tbsp. lime juice (or lemon juice)
1/4 tsp. sea salt (or, to taste)
3/4 cup coconut milk

1 large bunch fresh baby spinach, washed thoroughly,
   blotted or spun dried, and broken into pieces
1/2 cup dry roasted peanuts, finely ground

1. Heat skillet to medium and season with oil. Sauté garlic
   gently for 2 to 3 minutes and remove from heat. Add remaining sauce ingredients.
2. Toss spinach and sauce together, then garnish with peanuts.
   Serve at once.

Chili, lime juice, peanuts, and coconut milk make this a South Seas favorite. You can use any raw or cooked green that you desire. If you love Thai food, this could become a favorite.

Guardian Angel,
please help me know
that I am one
with "All That Is,"
seen and unseen.

Raw Asparagus Salad with Dijon Vinaigrette

serves 4

The finest chefs of Europe have created incredible, complicated dishes around this wonderful shoot, but very few have considered preparing it in its natural state—raw! It is divine simply marinated for an hour or two and served in regal glory!

Guardian Angel, please help me take the time to appreciate the wonders of nature.

Dijon Vinaigrette Dressing:
1/2 Tbsp. lime juice or wine vinegar
1 Tbsp. flax oil or extra-virgin olive oil
1 Tbsp. water
1/2 clove garlic, crushed
1 tsp. shallots, minced
1 tsp. dijon-style prepared mustard
1/8 tsp. powdered dry mustard (Colemans®)
1/4 tsp. salt
freshly ground pepper

1 large bunch fresh asparagus (about 2 1/2 lbs.)
1/2 head of green-leaf lettuce, washed and dried

1. Prepare dressing and set aside.
2. To prepare asparagus, wash and trim bottom ends. Using a potato peeler, remove skins beginning halfway down the stalk to the ends.
3. Marinate asparagus in dressing for 1 to 2 hours in an airtight container in the refrigerator.
4. Serve asparagus chilled, on a bed of green-leaf lettuce.

Insights: Choose asparagus that is firm, with straight green stalks and tips that are well formed and tightly closed. Store in a covered container in the refrigerator until ready to use. (Do not wash before storing.) Use as soon after purchasing as possible. To perk up slightly limp asparagus, trim bottom ends and stand in cold water for an hour or so before storing in refrigerator.

Italian Mushroom Leek Salad

serves 4

Pesto Salad Dressing:
1 Tbsp. *Pesto* (see pg. 70) or fresh minced basil
1/4 cup purified water
1 Tbsp. lemon juice
1 tsp. Braggs Liquid Aminos® (or, to taste)

2 cups mushrooms, cleaned and thinly sliced
1/2 leek, washed well and sliced paper thin, crosswise
1 head of radicchio lettuce or 1/2 head red-leaf lettuce,
    washed and dried

1. Mix *Dressing* ingredients together and set aside.
2. Combine mushrooms and leeks, and toss gently. Set aside.
3. Pour dressing over mushroom-leek mixture and toss again.
4. Serve on a bed of radicchio lettuce or red-leaf lettuce.

Insights: Leeks resemble giant green onions and are great raw, sliced thinly in salads, or cooked in vegetable dishes, grains, and soups. It's important to take the time to clean them well, since dirt accumulates in the interlocking leaves. Gently peel back each leaf a couple of inches to wash, or slice it lengthwise and carefully disassemble.

Raw mushrooms and leeks are perfect together, served simply on a bed of colorful radicchio lettuce. It's proof positive that food can be easy to prepare and still be a gourmet delight!

Guardian Angel, please help me align myself with the Truth and the Love of God.

Our angels guided us to a wonderful vegan restaurant while we were exploring the Caribbean island of Martinique. The surprising salad we had there delighted us so that I copied it as soon as we returned home and have made it many times since. It's fat-free and amazingly simple!

Guardian Angel,
please help me
maintain harmony
in my thoughts,
and my life.

Caribbean Grated Vegetable Salad

serves 4

Caribbean Lime Dressing:
2 Tbsp. fresh lime juice
6 Tbsp. water
1 green onion, thinly sliced
1 small clove garlic, crushed
1/4 tsp. maple syrup
pinch sea salt (or, to taste)

2 cups beets, shredded
2 cups chayote squash, peeled, seeded, and shredded
2 cups icicle radish, shredded
2 cups West Indian pumpkin or butternut squash, seeded, peeled, and shredded
2 cups yam, peeled and shredded

1. Combine ingredients for *Dressing* and set aside.
2. Attractively arrange grated vegetables on individual salad plates by placing 1/2 cup of beets in a small pile in the center of each. Place 1/2 cup pumpkin on one side and 1/2 cup yam on the other. Then put 1/2 cup chayote and 1/2 cup icicle radish on the other two sides.
3. Serve at room temperature, or slightly chilled, with the *Dressing* drizzled over the salad.

Balinese Vegetable, Noodle & Peanut Salad

serves 4

4 ounces chow mein, udon noodles or linguine, cooked
   according to package directions

Balinese Peanut Dressing:
2 Tbsp. creamy peanut butter
1 Tbsp. tamari soy sauce
1 clove garlic, crushed
1/4 tsp. fresh ground chili paste
1 Tbsp. pure maple syrup (or Sucanat®)
1 tsp. fresh ginger, peeled and grated
1 Tbsp. lime juice (or lemon juice)
2 Tbsp. water

Salad:
1 cup carrots, shredded
1 cup fresh bean sprouts
1 cup Asian or Napa cabbage, cut into shreds
2 green onions, sliced
1 cup pressed or baked seasoned tofu, cut julienne-style
1 cup fresh cilantro (Chinese parsley), chopped
1/4 cup roasted peanuts, chopped

1. Cook noodles according to package directions, rinse in cold
   water, and allow to remain in ice water to prevent noodles from
   sticking together. Set aside.
2. Combine ingredients for dressing in a blender and purée.
3. Drain the noodles and toss with vegetables, tofu, and dressing.
   Serve at room temperature or slightly chilled, garnished with
   peanuts.

Creamy, spicy, sweet and pungent, this salad will transport you to the South Seas island of Bali! We enjoy this as a delicious lunch or dinner for two, but it can also be served as a luscious first course for four.

Guardian Angel,
please help me
strive for a feeling
of oneness
with the Creator.

Orange blossom water is a fragrant essence often used in Moroccan and Middle Eastern cooking. If you don't find it available in your neck of the woods, orange extract is a suitable substitute.

Guardian Angel,
please help me
see my affinity
with all life.

Moroccan Beets in
Orange Blossom Dressing
serves 4

4 beets, peeled, sliced 1/2-inch thick, and steamed
1/4 cup onion, finely minced
1/2 cup parsley, minced
1/2 cup orange juice
1 tsp. orange blossom water (or 1/8 tsp. orange extract)
1 tsp. Sucanat® (dehydrated sugar cane juice)
sea salt and pepper to taste

1 head bibb lettuce

1. Combine all ingredients, except lettuce; toss and chill for at least 1 hour.
2. To serve, arrange lettuce on individual plates and pile beets in the center.

Insights: Parsley is the most commonly used of all the leafy herbs. Curly-leafed parsley can hide dirt and sand, so wash it carefully and dry it between towels or in a salad spinner. Save the stems to add to soup broth or to use in making vegetable juice. It adds a fresh green taste and is high is vitamins A and C, as well as iron and potassium.

Moroccan Carrots with Cinnamon & Orange Blossoms

serves 4

2 medium carrots, grated
1/4 cup orange juice
2 tsp. brown rice syrup
1 tsp. cinnamon
1 tsp. orange blossom water (or 1/8 tsp. orange extract)
pinch of sea salt
1 head bibb lettuce
a few orange blossoms

1. Combine all ingredients, except lettuce, and chill for 1 hour.
2. Serve on a bed of lettuce, garnished with orange blossoms, chilled or at room temperature.

Insights: Edible flowers make fragrant and beautiful garnishes. Be sure to use unsprayed flowers from your garden or the market. Some of the more popular varieties are nasturtiums, geraniums, rose petals, pansies, violets, marigolds, lobelia, and chive flowers.

The flavor of cinnamon and orange blossoms lend themselves beautifully to the natural sweetness of root vegetables. This is colorful and delicious served alongside *Moroccan Beets*. (See opposite page.)

*Guardian Angel,
please help me
hear your messages of
love, peace, and joy.*

An Arabic friend taught me how to prepare this incredibly delicious traditional eggplant salad. I have toned down some of the spices to suit our more delicate tastes, but otherwise it's right out of the Arabian Nights!

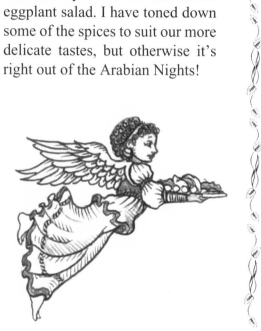

Guardian Angel,
please help me
be peaceful in
the knowledge that
all my needs
will be provided for.

Arabian Eggplant Salad
serves 4–6

1 large eggplant, sliced lengthwise 1/2-inch thick
olive oil cooking spray
1 tomato, minced

Arabic Salad Dressing:
1/2 Tbsp. flax oil or extra-virgin olive oil
1 Tbsp. water
1 Tbsp. balsamic vinegar
1 Tbsp. tomato paste
1 clove garlic, crushed
2 Tbsp. parsley, chopped
2 Tbsp. fresh cilantro (Chinese parsley), chopped
1/2 tsp. ground turmeric
1/2 tsp. ground cumin
1/2 tsp. paprika
1/8 tsp. ground cayenne
1/4 tsp. sea salt (or, to taste)

4 cups baby lettuce mix

1. Lightly spray eggplant slices on both sides with oil. Place on a broiler pan and roast in oven until soft, about 20 minutes. Remove and allow to cool. Mince eggplant.
2. Combine *Dressing* ingredients, and mix well. Add eggplant, toss, and chill for 1 to 2 hours.
3. Serve chilled eggplant salad over lettuce leaves.

Yugoslavian Eggplant & Pepper Salad

serves 4

1 large eggplant
1/2 red bell pepper, seeded and diced
1/2 green bell pepper, seeded and diced
1 clove garlic, crushed
2 Tbsp. lime or lemon juice
1/4 cup parsley, minced
1 Tbsp. flax oil or extra-virgin olive oil
2 Tbsp. water
1 green onion, thinly sliced
1/2 tsp. sea salt (or, to taste)
freshly ground pepper to taste
1 head endive or baby lettuce mix, washed, dried, and
    broken into pieces

1. Slice eggplant in half lengthwise and rub oil on the cut sides.
   Place in 400 degree oven for 45 minutes or until the inside
   is soft and the skin is charred.
2. Carefully remove the skin of the eggplant and discard. Cut
   flesh into small cubes.
3. Combine with remaining ingredients, except lettuce, and
   toss gently. Chill for at least 1 hour.
4. To serve, arrange lettuce on salad plates and spoon eggplant
   mixture on top.

Eggplant and bell peppers are cousins, both belonging to the family of nightshades. In this Northern European salad they unite to form a lovely marriage of texture and taste!

*Guardian Angel,
please help me
extend the gift of
free will to everyone.*

Unique in flavor and texture, this naturally sweet salad is a gourmet delight! It's as perfect served as a first course as it is at the end of a meal.

*Guardian Angel,
please help me
experience the pure
joy of loving.*

Apple-Fennel Salad with Poppy Seed Dressing

serves 4

Poppy Seed Dressing:
1/4 cup fresh orange juice
1 tsp. zest (shredded peel) of organically grown orange
1 Tbsp. flax oil or extra-virgin olive oil
1 tsp. poppy seeds
1/4 tsp. Spike® seasoning

2–3 red apples, cored and diced
1 medium bulb fennel, remove tough outer stalk and julienne
1/4 small red onion, julienned (see pg. 55)
2 cups arugula or other bitter green, washed and dried

1. Combine ingredients for dressing and mix well.
2. Toss together all ingredients, except greens.
3. Arrange *Apple-Fennel Salad* on top of greens and serve.

Sunchoke Salad with Creamy Garlic-Ginger Dressing

serves 4

Creamy Garlic-Ginger Dressing:
1/4 cup *Roasted Garlic Cheese Spread* (see pg. 73)
6 Tbsp. purified water
1 Tbsp. tamari soy sauce or light miso paste
1 Tbsp. lemon juice or rice vinegar
1/2 tsp. fresh grated ginger
1/2 tsp. powdered dry mustard (Colemans®)

4 cups sunchokes (Jerusalem artichokes), cleaned and sliced
1/2 small red onion, julienned (see pg. 55)
4 cups fresh young spinach or sunflower greens

1. Combine ingredients for dressing and set aside.
2. Combine remaining ingredients, except greens, and toss well.
3. Arrange greens on individual plates, place salad on top, and
   serve.

Sunchokes, sometimes called Jerusalem Artichokes, are roots that taste very much like the hearts of artichokes. They can be steamed, sauteed, or eaten raw as called for in this simple recipe.

*Guardian Angel,
please help me
have a sense of
contentment
with who I am.*

Mexican cuisine is far more diverse than one would guess. Beans and peas of all kinds are available in the public markets where produce is lovingly arranged by color. This lentil salad embodies the flavor of Mexico with its fragrant cilantro, oregano, and peppers. Viva Mexico!

Guardian Angel,
please help me
hear, see, and speak
with a peaceful heart.

Mexican Lentil Salad

serves 4

2 cups cooked, drained lentils (or lentil sprouts)
1 carrot, shredded or julienned
1 large tomato, seeded and diced
1 long green (California or Anaheim) chili, seeded and diced
1 cup red onions, thinly sliced
1 stalk celery, thinly sliced
2 Tbsp. cilantro (Chinese parsley), minced
1 Tbsp. green onions, thinly sliced
1 Tbsp. lime juice
1 Tbsp. flax oil or extra-virgin olive oil
1/2 tsp. crushed oregano
1/4 tsp. paprika or chili powder (to taste)
sea salt and pepper to taste
4 cups baby greens, sunflower greens, or spinach, washed, dried, and broken into pieces

1. Combine lentils, vegetables and herbs in a bowl and toss.
2. Mix remaining ingredients together and pour over salad. Toss again and serve on a bed of greens, chilled or at room temperature.

Basque Fava Bean & Herb Salad

serves 4

4 cups cooked, shelled fava beans
1/3 cup red onion, minced
2 Tbsp. fresh oregano, minced
2 Tbsp. fresh basil, minced
1 Tbsp. flax oil or extra-virgin olive oil
1 Tbsp. lime juice or balsamic vinegar
sea salt and pepper to taste
1 head romaine lettuce, washed, dried, and torn into
   pieces

1. Combine all ingredients, except lettuce, and toss well. Allow to marinate for at least 1 hour prior to serving.
2. Serve over lettuce, chilled or at room temperature.

Insights: Oregano is a very aromatic and strong herb. It's used widely in Mexico, Italy, Spain, and other Mediterranean countries and is known for its slightly bitter, but pleasant taste. Use it sparingly, as it can take over the flavor of other foods. If a recipe calls for 1 teaspoon of dried oregano, substitute 1 tablespoon of fresh, minced.

In the mountains of the Pyrenees they say that if you're not eating beans with every meal, your not eating Basque food. This delicious savory salad will fulfill that requirement and more!

Guardian Angel, please help me open my mind to inspiration from the Celestial Realms.

Peas of many kinds find their way into the cuisine of the Caribbean. I especially like this spicy salad of black-eyed peas, which I once tasted in Runaway Bay on the island of Jamaica!

Guardian Angel, please help me know that I am unique and greatly loved.

Jamaican Black-Eyed Pea Salad

serves 4–6

2 cups sprouted or cooked black-eyed peas
3 green onions, thinly sliced
2 cloves garlic, crushed
1 large sweet red pepper, diced
2 Tbsp. fresh jalapeno peppers, seeded and finely minced
1 1/2 Tbsp. lime or lemon juice
1 Tbsp. flax or extra-virgin olive oil
1 Tbsp. water
1/2 tsp. sea salt (or, to taste)
2 cups per serving mixed baby lettuce or sunflower
   greens
freshly ground black pepper

1. Toss black-eyed peas and other ingredients, except lettuce, together and allow to rest for at least 15 minutes.
2. Place lettuce on individual serving plates and heap black-eyed peas in center.
3. Generously grind fresh pepper on top.

Insights: Hot chili peppers require careful handling. Never touch your eyes, rub sensitive areas, or handle children or pets after touching them, until you have washed your hands thoroughly. Much of the heat is contained in the seeds and membranes, so slice peppers lengthwise and remove those. The longer minced pepper sits in a recipe, the hotter the mixture becomes; so if you are preparing a recipe in advance, you may wish to use less chili or add it just prior to serving.

Fresh Peas in Avocado Mayonnaise

serves 4

Avocado Mayonnaise:
2 Tbsp. purified water
1/2 avocado, peeled and mashed
1 Tbsp. lemon or lime juice
1 Tbsp. shallots or green onions, minced
1 tsp. Vege-Sal® (or, to taste)

1 cup fresh peas or sprouted peas
4 fresh mushrooms, wiped clean and julienned
1 small tomato, seeded and diced
1/2 small cucumber, seeded and diced
4 cups baby lettuce mix or sunflower greens, washed and
   dried.

1. Combine ingredients for *Avocado Mayonnaise*, and mix well.
2. Add remaining ingredients, except lettuce, and toss gently.
3. Arrange lettuce attractively on individual plates and heap
   pea mixture on top.

Insights: If a cucumber is organically grown, the skin is edible; otherwise, I suggest peeling it using a potato peeler. To remove the seeds, slice it in half lengthwise. Using a sharp paring knife, slice along the edge of the seeds on both sides. With a spoon, dislodge the seedbed by running the spoon down under the seeds along the length of the cucumber. If desired, save the seeds for use in making fresh vegetable juice.

R aw or sprouted peas are just naturally sweet and crunchy and add a delightful contrast to the creaminess of avocado. It's lovely over lettuce or as a filling in tomatoes. Frozen peas can be used if fresh are unavailable.

Guardian Angel,
please help me
see myself
as you see me,
whole and perfect.

Chapter Seven

Celestial Soups

A Talk with Spirit about Trust

Energies of Light, please assist me in knowing that the universe supports me in becoming all that I am capable of being. Help me to feel secure even when I am challenged and to understand that all lessons are opportunities for spiritual growth. Help nurture trust within me, so I can learn to be comfortable with the process of life and its many ebbs and tides. Please help me learn that I can trust in your guidance to assist me throughout my life.

I know that this food is a beautiful gift of life, and I am filled with gratitude for the opportunity to merge its vibrational essence with my own. I trust that it will provide me with good health and well-being. I love you, I bless you, I am one with you and All That Is.

Recipes at a Glance

Celestial Soups

These quick and easy blender soups are great for lunch or dinner. Fresh sprouted peas lend a lovely garden flavor to this unusual, creamy pea soup. The cooked peas and apples add a gentle sweetness that make it one of my favorites.

Guardian Angel,
please help me sense
your Divine Presence.

Vitality Soup

serves 2 (full meal)

1 1/2 cups fresh vegetable juice or *Rejuvilac* (see pg. 15)
6 ounces greens (spinach, sunflower, buckwheat, etc.)
1 medium papaya, pear, or apple, quartered and cored
1/2–1 medium avocado, quartered, peeled, and pitted
1/4 cup young pea or mixed bean sprouts (see pg. 9)
1/8–1/4 tsp. ground kelp or dulse
1/4 cup pumpkin or sunflower sprouts (see pg. 8)
2 tsp. nutritional yeast
1/2 tsp. unpasteurized light miso

1. Combine all ingredients in a blender and purée until smooth.
2. Serve at room temperature or warm to 115 degrees.

Sprouted Pea Soup

serves 4

2 cups young sprouted peas (see pg. 9)
1 cup frozen peas
1/2–1 avocado or 8–12 soaked almonds (24-hour soak)
1 medium apple, peeled, cored, and shredded
1 1/2 cups water
1/2 tsp. unpasteurized light miso
pinch of dill weed
sea salt or Braggs Liquid Aminos® to taste

1. Combine all ingredients in blender and purée until smooth.
2. Strain mixture and serve at room temperature, or warm to 115 degrees.

Cream of Pumpkin Soup

serves 4

6 cups pumpkin, peeled, seeded, and shredded
3/4 cup *Almond Cream* (see pg. 16)
1 cup purified water
1 green onion, sliced
pinch of nutmeg

1. Combine all ingredients in a blender and purée until smooth.
2. Serve at room temperature or warm to 115 degrees.

Yummy Yam Soup

serves 4

2 cups yams, peeled and shredded
2 ears fresh corn, kernels removed from cob
1/2–1 avocado
1 tsp. unpasteurized light miso

1. Combine ingredients in a blender and purée until smooth, adding water to achieve desired consistency.
2. Serve at room temperature or warm to 115 degrees.

The smooth lushness of *Almond Cream* makes this pumpkin soup an exquisite and satisfying lunch or first course. Serve it at any temperature—it is wonderful! Raw soups are great chilled on a summer day or slightly warmed in winter.

Guardian Angel, please help me acknowledge inner truth and guidance.

Brilliant gold with specks of red and yellow make this a feast for the eyes as well as the palate! It's really a culinary delight!

Guardian Angel, please help me become the essence of who I truly am.

Sunny Carrot Soup

serves 4

3 cups fresh carrot juice
1 Tbsp. light miso paste (or, to taste)
1/2 tsp. Braggs Liquid Aminos® (or, to taste)
1 small clove garlic, crushed (or 1/4 tsp. garlic powder)
2 tsp. fresh basil or 1/2 tsp. dried crushed basil
1 avocado, peeled, seeded, and diced
3 plum tomatoes, peeled, seeded, and diced
2 ears sweet corn, husked and kernels removed from cob
1 Tbsp. minced red onion
1 Tbsp. fresh cilantro, chopped

1. Put carrot juice, miso, Braggs®, garlic powder, and basil in a blender. Add half of the avocado, tomatoes, and corn kernels, and purée.
2. Combine remaining vegetables, except cilantro, and toss.
3. To serve, pour puréed mixture into individual bowls and stir in tossed vegetables. Serve chilled, at room temperature, or warmed to 115 degrees. Garnish with cilantro.

Curried Carrot Soup

serves 4

2 cups fresh carrot juice
2 cups thick *Cashew* or *Almond Cream* (see pg. 16, 17)
1 plum tomato, peeled and seeded
1 Tbsp. light miso paste (or, to taste)
1/2 Tbsp. mild curry powder
1/2 small zucchini or yellow crookneck squash, diced
1/4 red bell pepper, minced
2 Tbsp. minced red onion
1 Tbsp. fresh chervil, chopped

1. Combine carrot juice, cream, tomato, miso, and curry in a blender and purée.
2. Combine remaining ingredients, except chervil, and toss.
3. To serve, pour puréed mixture into individual bowls and stir in tossed vegetables. Serve chilled, at room temperature, or gently heated. Garnish with chervil.

Insights: Chervil should always be added at the end of cooking time, or as a garnish, to retain its beauty and aroma. Its lacy leaves dry out easily and, when cooked, lose their flavor. As a garnish, chervil adds a delicate taste and aroma akin to anise, but almost peppery. Enjoy it also in salads and dressings.

Fragrant and delightful, this soup is a wonderful way to get your beta-carotene! Since curry is actually a blend of spices, different brands will lend entirely different tastes to your soup. Some are spicy and others are sweet, so try several blends to discover your favorites.

Guardian Angel, please help me live life peacefully and with presence of mind.

This South American-inspired soup is lovely to look at and heavenly to taste. Gently cooking the onions, which would otherwise overtake the flavor, is the secret!

Guardian Angel, please help me recognize that I am capable of greatness.

South American Corn Soup

serves 4

1/2 white onion, diced
2 cups combination cucumber-celery-cabbage juice
2 ears white corn, removed from cob
1 tomato, seeded and diced
1 Tbsp. minced cilantro

1. Heat 1/2 cup of juice in skillet and add onions. Cook onions gently until they are transparent, about 8 minutes.
2. Allow onions to cool slightly. Place them, along with the remaining juice and corn, into a blender; purée until smooth.
3. Serve soup at room temperature or warmed to 115 degrees. Garnish with cilantro and tomatoes.

Insights: To remove corn kernels from the cob, first peel off the husk and remove the silk. Holding the corn vertically over a platter, position a sharp knife between the corn and the cob and slice downward. Be careful not to cut into the cob. To remove the precious corn "nubs," use an inverted spoon and scrape down the sides of the cob, catching the "nubs" inside the spoon.

Iowa Corn Chowder

serves 4

olive oil cooking spray or 1/2 tsp. olive oil
1 onion, diced
1 large potato, peeled and diced
2 stalks celery, diced
1/4 green bell pepper, diced
1/4 red bell pepper, diced
1 bay leaf
2 cups purified water
1/4 cup unbleached flour
2 cups plain soy milk
1/4 cup *Cashew Cream* (see pg. 17)
1 tsp. sea salt (or, to taste)
2 ears fresh corn kernels, removed from cob
freshly ground pepper to taste

1. Heat soup kettle to medium and season with oil. Sauté onion until transparent, about 5 minutes, adding small amounts of water, if needed, to prevent sticking.
2. Add celery, red and green peppers, potatoes, bay leaf, and water. Simmer until potatoes are tender, about 15 minutes.
3. Mix flour with 1 cup of milk until it is smooth and free of lumps. Add it to the pot, along with the remaining soy milk, *Cashew Cream,* and salt, and allow it to simmer for a few minutes until thickened.
4. Stir in the corn and heat gently.
5. Add freshly ground pepper and serve.

Naturally sweet and creamy, this tasty corn chowder is always a winner. This version is enriched with the addition of *Cashew Cream,* but you can also use commercial tofu cream cheese or puréed tofu.

*Guardian Angel,
please help me see
all the world
as living Light.*

Yam and corn are two ingredients most people don't think of eating raw, but they are exquisite together!

The delicate flavors of fennel and dill also combine beautifully with the richness of cashew cream in this luscious *Cucumber Bisque*.

*Guardian Angel,
please help me achieve
a quiet mind
and a loving heart.*

Ginger-Curry Corn Soup

serves 4

1 cup yams or butternut squash, peeled and shredded
3 ears fresh corn, kernels removed from cob
1 tsp. unpasteurized light miso (or, to taste)
1/2 tsp. curry powder
1/2 tsp. freshly ground ginger root

1. Combine ingredients in a blender and purée until smooth, adding water to achieve desired consistency.
2. Serve at room temperature or warm to 115 degrees.

Cucumber Bisque

serves 4

2 cucumbers, peeled, seeded, and chopped
1 cup fennel bulb, peeled and chopped
1 zucchini, chopped
1/2 avocado, peeled and chopped
1/4 cup *Cashew Cream* (see pg. 17)
1 Tbsp. red onion
1 Tbsp. unpasteurized light miso (or, to taste)
1 tsp. ground coriander
1/2 tsp. dried dill weed
1–2 cups purified water
1 green onion, sliced
1 Tbsp. mint, slivered

1. Combine ingredients, except green onion and mint, in a blender and purée until smooth and creamy, adding water to achieve desired consistency.
2. Pour into individual bowls and garnish with mint and green onion. Serve chilled.

Gazpacho
(Spanish Chilled Tomato Soup)

serves 4

4–6 ripe tomatoes, diced
1 medium stalk celery, diced
1/2 cucumber, peeled, seeded, and diced
1/4 bell pepper, diced
4 radishes, thinly sliced
1 green onion, thinly sliced
2 Tbsp. parsley, minced
4 tsp. lemon juice
2 tsp. flax oil or extra-virgin olive oil
1 tsp. sea salt (or, to taste)
freshly ground pepper
1 avocado, peeled, seeded, and cut into small cubes (cut
    just prior to serving)
1/4 cup young sunflower seed sprouts (see pg. 8) or
    Seasoned Sunflower Seeds (see pg. 65)

1. Combine all ingredients, except avocado and sunflower seed
   sprouts and mix well.
2. Purée half the tomato mixture in a blender or food processor.
3. Return the puréed mixture to the original mixture and stir.
4. If possible, cover, and allow to chill in the refrigerator for
   one hour.
5. Prior to serving, cut the avocado into cubes and fold into the
   Gazpacho. Serve in chilled bowls and garnish with sprouts.

This version of the traditional Spanish soupy salad is thick and chunky. Blending only half the ingredients is the secret. The avocado makes it extra rich and delicious!

*Guardian Angel,
please help me accept
the gifts of life
graciously.*

Nurturing and nourishing, this delicious, warm broth is great on a cold day or when you feel under the weather. It's also very good after a cleansing diet or fast to keep the tummy from rebelling against heavier foods.

*Guardian Angel,
please help me let go
of limiting thoughts
and behaviors.*

Miso Shiro
(Japanese Cultured Soybean Soup)
serves 4

1 quart *Shiitake Dashi* (see pg. 133)
1/4 cup hatcho miso or 1/2 cup mellow light or red miso
1–2 ounces tofu, cut into 1/2 inch cubes (optional)
1 green onion, thinly sliced
a few strips of kombu or wakame seaweed

1. Place *Shiitake Dashi* in a pot and bring it to simmer. Remove 1 cup dashi, cool to 115 degrees (warm to the touch) and mix in miso until smooth and creamy. Set aside.
2. Add tofu to pot and remove from heat. Cool to 115 degrees. Return miso-dashi mixture to pot. Be careful: overcooking will destroy the friendly microorganisms and enzymes in the miso.
3. Serve in small individual serving dishes. Garnish with green onion and a strip or two of seaweed.

Variations: Add any of the following ingredients –
Decoratively cut pieces of daikon radish or turnip
Agé (fried tofu) or seitan (wheatmeat or wheat gluten)
Sliced fresh white, shiitake or enouki mushrooms
Small pieces of spinach or Napa cabbage
Decoratively cut pieces of cooked carrot or sweet potato
Cooked soba noodles or bean threads
Fresh bean sprouts
Snow peas

Japanese Rice & Seaweed Soup

serves 4

4 cups hot cooked brown rice
1 quart hot *Shiitake Dashi* (see pg. 133)
1 tsp. wasabi (powdered Japanese horseradish), mixed
   with 2 Tbsp. water
tamari soy sauce or miso to taste
3 sheets nori seaweed, cut into strips
1 Tbsp. toasted sesame seeds

1. Combine first 5 ingredients in soup pot and gently heat to
   115 degrees.
2. Pour into individual serving bowls and garnish with sesame
   seeds. Serve warm.

Insights: It's easy to cook fluffy brown rice every time.
Measure the rice, rinse it well, and allow it to drain in a mesh
colander. Cover with 1 1/2 times purified water (1 cup rice
to 1 1/2 cups water) and bring to a boil. Reduce to a gentle
simmer and cover with a tight-fitting lid. Cook undisturbed
for 50 minutes. Turn off heat and leave it alone for another
10 minutes. Do not lift the lid or stir the rice while it's
cooking. Basmati rice requires about 10 minutes less
cooking time, so adjust timing as needed.

Simple and nurturing, this Japanese soup is a good way to use leftover rice. It makes a great first course for *Sunomono* (see pg. 87) and a variety of *Japanese Sushimaki* (see pg. 166).

*Guardian Angel,
please help me
open my heart
and mind
to All That Is.*

I discovered miso ramen at one of the many noodle shops in Tokyo and it has become my favorite winter soup! There is something very nurturing about noodles and gently cooked veggies in miso broth that is especially wonderful on cold nights!

Guardian Angel,
please help me
let go of fear
and base my decisions
on Love and Light.

Miso Ramen
(Japanese Vegetable Noodle Soup)
serves 4

12 ounces Chinese noodles, cooked according to package
   directions

6–8 dried shiitake mushrooms, soaked in 2 cups hot
   purified water for 20 minutes
1 medium onion, cut julienne-style (see pg. 55)
2 cloves garlic, minced olive oil cooking spray or 1/2 tsp.
   sesame oil
10–12 medium fresh mushrooms, quartered
2 carrots, sliced
1 small green pepper, cut julienne-style
1/2 small Napa or Asian cabbage, sliced crosswise

olive oil cooking spray or 1/2 tsp. sesame oil
1 pound tofu, cut into 1-inch cubes
1 qt. purified water
reserved shiitake-soaking liquid

6 Tbsp. unpasteurized hatcho miso (or any dark miso)
4 green onions, sliced at an angle into 1-inch lengths,
dash of assorted chili pepper seasoning

1. After cooking noodles, drain water and set noodles aside.
2. Remove stems from soaked shiitake mushrooms and discard. Slice mushrooms julienne style. Set aside. (Remember to reserve the shiitake soaking liquid.)

3. Heat a non-stick skillet or wok to medium and season with a spray of oil or 1/2 tsp. oil. Sauté onions and garlic until transparent, about 5 minutes, adding small amounts of water, if needed, to prevent sticking. Add mushrooms and cook another 5 minutes. Add cabbage and green peppers and cook until cabbage is wilted.

4. While vegetables are cooking, heat another non-stick skillet and season with a spray of olive oil cooking spray or remaining 1/2 tsp. oil. Fry tofu, turning as needed, until all sides are golden brown.

5. Combine reserved shiitake soaking liquid with enough water to equal 5 cups and bring to a simmer. Remove 1 cup of hot liquid, cool, and mix miso into it until smooth and creamy. Add sautéed vegetables and tofu to simmering pot. Remove from heat and allow to cool to 115 degrees. Return miso to pot.

6. While soup is cooling bring a quart of water to boil in a kettle. Dip the precooked noodles into the hot water to warm them.

7. To serve, warm soup slightly, if needed. Divide the noodles into separate bowls and ladle vegetables and broth over the top. Garnish with green onions and pepper seasoning.

Insights: Miso is a delicious, salty tasting, fermented soybean paste or soy and grain paste combination, containing friendly bacteria that is healing to the digestive tract. The flavor varies greatly, with the lighter miso being the mildest in taste, while the darker varieties are more robust. Use it generously in soups, sauces, dressings, and grain dishes.

There are many varieties of Asian noodles, so choose your favorite. We like Ramen, Somen, and Udon noodles best for this recipe.

Guardian Angel, please help me make decisions that serve my highest good.

The flavor and texture of mushrooms add a gourmet quality to this favorite Asian soup that is almost never offered without meat. Sesame oil, chili paste and cilantro combine to make this broth outstanding! It's light and yet aromatic with an unmistakable Asian flavor.

Guardian Angel, please assist me in allowing health to reign supreme in my body.

Mushroom Won Ton (Chinese Dumpling Soup)

serves 4

4 dried shiitake mushrooms, soaked in 2 cups warm water for 20 minutes
olive oil cooking spray or 1/2 tsp. toasted sesame oil
1 medium clove garlic, crushed
1/2 lb. fresh mushrooms, minced
1/2 tsp. arrowroot (or cornstarch) in 1 Tbsp. water
2 green onions, thinly sliced
1 1/2 tsp. soy sauce
16 won ton wrappers
2 Tbsp. flour + 3 Tbsp. water, mixed to form a thick paste
6–8 cups boiling water

Broth:
reserved shiitake mushroom-soaking liquid + enough water to equal 2 cups
1 Tbsp. Aji Mirin® rice wine
1 Tbsp. tamari soy sauce
1 Tbsp. vegetarian "chicken-flavored" broth powder
1 tsp. maple syrup (or other sweetener)
1/4 tsp. toasted sesame oil
1/8 tsp. chili paste
2 green onions, thinly sliced
1/2 cup cilantro (Chinese parsley leaves)

1. Heat skillet to medium-hot and add a spray of oil or 1/2 teaspoon oil. Add crushed garlic and sauté for one minute.

2. Add fresh, minced mushrooms to skillet and continue cooking until almost dry, stirring frequently for about 7 or 8 minutes. Add small amounts of water, if needed, to prevent sticking.

3. Meanwhile, remove shiitake mushrooms from soaking-water and reserve liquid. Cut off and discard stems, and mince mushrooms.

4. When fresh mushrooms have cooked, add shiitake mushrooms and arrowroot and mix well. Cook another minute and add green onion and soy sauce. Remove from skillet and allow to cool to room temperature. Roughly divide into 16 portions.

5. Mix flour paste in small bowl and place near work area.

6. Lay four won ton wrappers on clean, dry work surface. Brush the edges of each won ton wrapper with flour paste.

7. Place one portion of filling in the center of each wrapper.

8. Fold wrappers diagonally in half, over the filling, forming triangles. Press along edges to seal.

9. Take the two opposite corners of each triangle and tuck one under the other, pinching to seal, and form the shape of a nurse's cap. Place all four filled won tons on waxed paper and cover with a clean, damp towel. Repeat steps 6–9 to complete filling remaining won ton.

10. When all 16 won tons are completed, gently place them in boiling water and cook until tender, about 6 minutes.

11. While won tons are cooking, combine *Broth* ingredients and bring to a simmer.

12. Divide *Broth* into four soup bowls, add cooked won tons, and serve, garnished with cilantro.

If you are serving this to guests, prepare the filling and broth in advance and fill the wrappers as close as possible to arrival time. Then, 10 minutes prior to serving, boil water, cook the won tons, and reheat the broth.

Guardian Angel, please help me see that this world is miraculous beyond description.

If you like mushrooms, you'll love the rich intensity of this creamy, delicious soup. We prefer to use porcini, shiitaki, and morels, but any single variety will send you to mushroom heaven.

Guardian Angel, please help me see spiritual luminosity emanating from everyone and everything.

Swiss Cream of Mushroom Soup

serves 4

1 cup dehydrated mushrooms of choice, soaked in warm
  water for 1/2 hour
olive oil cooking spray or 1/2 tsp. olive oil
1 large leek, washed thoroughly and sliced
1 lb. fresh mushrooms, chopped
2 Tbsp. unbleached flour
1 Tbsp. powdered vegetarian "chicken-flavored" broth
1 qt. *Almond Milk* (see pg. 16), soy milk, or rice milk
2 Tbsp. light miso (or, to taste)
1/4 tsp. white pepper
2 Tbsp. sliced almonds
1 Tbsp. fresh chervil, chopped

1. While dehydrated mushrooms are soaking, heat a large non-stick soup pot and season with oil. Add leeks and cook for about 5 minutes, stirring, adding small amounts of water, if needed, to prevent sticking.
2. Add fresh mushrooms to the pot and cook for 5 minutes.
3. Sprinkle flour and broth powder into pot and stir well. Cook for 2 more minutes, stirring.
4. Add milk to pot, allowing it to come to a simmer, and reduce heat to maintain a gentle simmer.
5. Remove tough stems from reconstituted mushrooms and discard. Chop mushrooms and add to pot. Retain mushroom soaking liquid, carefully straining out any sand.
6. Simmer gently for 30 minutes, adding additional water, as needed, to form a thick broth. Remove from heat.
7. Combine 1/2 cup of reserved mushroom soaking liquid, miso, and pepper, and blend, using a small hand blender or whisk. Add to soup pot and stir.
8. Pour into bowls and garnish with almonds and chervil.

French Potato Leek Soup

serves 4

olive oil cooking spray or 1/2 tsp. olive oil
2 large leeks, washed thoroughly and sliced
    (discard toughest ends)
2 large white or red potatoes, peeled and chopped
6 cups purified water or *Vegetable Herb Broth* (see
    pg. 132)
1 Tbsp. white miso or 3/4 tsp. sea salt (or, to taste)
1/8 tsp. white pepper
pinch of nutmeg

1. Heat skillet to medium, season with oil and add leeks. Sauté gently until soft, about 6 to 7 minutes, adding small amounts of water, if needed, to prevent sticking.
2. Meanwhile, place potatoes and water or broth in a soup pot and bring to a boil. Reduce heat to simmer, cover, and cook until tender.
3. Put half of the leeks and half of the potatoes with some of the cooking broth in a blender and purée.
4. Force mixture through a sieve to strain out any rough pulp.
5. Return potato-leek mixture to soup pot and add all remaining ingredients. Bring soup to a gentle simmer and cook for 10 more minutes.

Potatoes and leeks are the perfect combo in this French version of potato soup. I especially like the chunks of potato and leek floating in the smooth puréed broth.

*Guardian Angel,
please help me heal my
body and mind
so that I may live in
harmony with Spirit.*

Hearty and nutritious, this Spanish-inspired stew is a satisfying meal in itself. If you prefer, you may use fava beans, great northern beans, or just about any variety you like in place of limas. It's great no matter what beans you use!

Guardian Angel, please help me hold the highest thoughts and emotions.

Basque Lima Bean & Potato Stew with Tempeh "Bacon"

serves 4

olive oil cooking spray or 1/2 tsp. olive oil
1 large onion, chopped
2 large potatoes, scrubbed well and cubed
2 cups cooked lima beans (see following *Insight*)
1–2 cups cabbage, sliced
2 cloves garlic, minced
1 tsp. paprika
1/8 tsp. Spanish saffron
1 tsp. sea salt (or, to taste)
freshly ground pepper
2–3 ounces *Tempeh "Bacon,"* minced (see following recipe)

1. Heat non-stick skillet to medium-hot and season with oil. Sauté onions until soft and transparent, adding small amounts of water, if needed, to prevent sticking. Add potatoes and enough water to cover, and bring to a boil. Simmer, covered, for 15 minutes.
2. Add remaining ingredients except salt, pepper and *Tempeh "Bacon."* Cover and continue cooking for another 15 to 20 minutes, or until potatoes are tender. If necessary, add additional water to maintain a liquid stew.
3. Season with salt and pepper to taste and garnish with *Tempeh "Bacon."* Serve hot.

Tempeh "Bacon"

makes 8 ounces

1/2 tsp. natural hickory smoke seasoning
2 Tbsp. tamari soy sauce
1 cup purified water
1 Tbsp. Sucanat® (dehydrated sugar cane juice)
2 cloves garlic, crushed
8 ounces tempeh, sliced into 1/4 inch strips

1. Combine ingredients and simmer for 20 minutes.
2. Preheat oven or grill to 400 degrees.
3. Grill or broil tempeh for 10 minutes, turning after 5 minutes, until brown on both sides.

Insights: Lima beans, like most other beans, require overnight or all-day soaking. Inspect them visually for dirt clumps and small rocks before rinsing thoroughly through a colander. Cover with 3 times the amount of water to beans and allow to soak until plump. They will triple in size. Drain and add purified water to cover. Bring to a boil and immediately reduce heat to a slow simmer to avoid the formation of foam. Cover, allowing a vent for steam to escape, and simmer for 2 to 3 hours, or until tender, checking every half hour to ensure that the water line has not dropped below the beans. Retain the vitamin-rich broth for use in soups.

A great commercial "bacon-flavored" product is Fakin' Bacon®, but if you prefer to make your own, or if it's not available in your health food store, this smokey tasting tempeh is great to use in TBLT's (*Tempeh "Bacon,"* lettuce, and tomato sandwiches), or as a garnish for soups and salads.

Guardian Angel, please help me develop strength, tenacity, and endurance.

No one can regulate this great Cuban export! The blend of seasonings here are unique and delicious. If you've never tasted black beans, you're in for a treat!

Guardian Angel, please help me act honorably with grace, humor, and wisdom.

Cuban Black Bean Soup

serves 4 to 6

olive oil cooking spray or 1/2 tsp. olive oil
1 medium onion, diced
2 cloves garlic, crushed
2 cups cooked black beans
1/2 tsp. ground cumin
dash of cayenne pepper
dash of allspice
1 Tbsp. dark miso or 1 tsp. sea salt (or, to taste)
1 medium carrot, diced
bean broth or *Vegetable Herb Broth* (see pg. 132)
1 ripe tomato, diced
1/2 cup cilantro (Chinese parsley), chopped

1. Heat non-stick soup kettle to medium-hot and season with oil. Sauté onion until light brown, adding small amounts of water, if needed, to prevent sticking. Add garlic and cook for 1 more minute.
2. Combine half the beans with half the onion and garlic mixture in a blender or food processor, along with a little water. Add the cumin, cayenne, allspice, and miso, and purée.
3. Combine ingredients, except tomatoes and cilantro, together in pot and add enough broth to achieve desired consistency. Cover and simmer for 30 to 45 minutes.
4. Garnish each bowl of soup with a little tomato and cilantro before serving.

Spanish Pea Soup

serves 4

olive oil cooking spray or 1/2 tsp. olive oil
1 medium onion, minced
1/2 carrot, minced
1 Tbsp. powdered vegetarian "chicken-flavored" broth
16 ounces frozen petite peas
1/4 tsp. ground basil (or 1 tsp. minced fresh basil leaves)
sea salt and ground pepper to taste
3 cups purified water

1. Heat a non-stick skillet to medium and season with oil. Sauté onions until soft, about 5 minutes, adding small amounts of water, if needed, to prevent sticking. Add carrots and cook another 5 minutes.
2. Place onion mixture and remaining ingredients in a blender or food processor and purée. Strain mixture through a wire strainer to remove pulp.
3. Pour mixture into soup pot, adding additional water, if needed, and simmer gently for 5 minutes. Serve hot.

Spanish-inspired pea soup can also be converted to fava or lima bean soup and is wonderful warmed or enjoyed at room temperature.

*Guardian Angel,
please help me
experience serenity
of spirit.*

The texture of barley is a welcome addition to this satisfying vegetable stew. Served with a salad, it's a meal in itself.

Guardian Angel, please help me be tolerant of the views of others.

Irish Vegetable Barley Stew

serves 8

1 qt. purified water
1 cup pearl barley
olive oil cooking spray or 1/2 tsp. toasted sesame oil
1 medium onion, chopped
3 cloves garlic, minced
2 cups lightly sprouted lentils (see pg. 9) or 3/4 cup
    lentils soaked in hot water for 30 minutes and drained
1 bay leaf
1 Tbsp. Italian seasoning
1 quart vegetable broth of choice (see pg. 132, 133)
4 cups fresh mushrooms, chopped
2 carrots, chopped
2 stalks celery, chopped
1/4 head cabbage or 1/4 bunch chard, chopped
1 Tbsp. powdered vegetarian "chicken-flavored" broth
2 Tbsp. dark miso paste
1 large tomato, seeded and diced

1. Bring 1 quart of water to a boil and add barley. Cover and reduce to a simmer.
2. Meanwhile, heat a non-stick pan to medium and season with oil. Add onion and garlic and cook until translucent, about 8 minutes, adding small amounts of water, if needed, to prevent sticking.
3. Add onion mixture, lentils, bay leaf, and Italian seasoning to a soup pot, and continue simmering, covered, for 40 minutes.
4. Add remaining ingredients, except miso and tomato, to pot. Return to simmer and cook another 15 minutes, or until barley, lentils, and vegetables are tender. Remove from heat.
5. Remove 1/2 cup of broth from soup and blend in miso using a small hand blender or whisk.
6. Add miso broth back to pot, stir in tomatoes, and serve.

Borscht (Russian Beet Soup)

serves 4

olive oil cooking spray or 1/2 tsp. olive oil
1 medium onion, diced
1 clove garlic, minced
1 carrot, diced
1 stalk celery, diced
4 cups *Vegetable Herb Broth* (see pg. 132)
1/2 pound beets, peeled and diced
1/2 tsp. brown rice syrup
1/2 tsp. sea salt (or, to taste)
3/4 cup *Tofu Sour Cream* (see recipe below)
2 tsp. fresh dill or chives, chopped

1. Heat soup kettle to medium and season with oil. Sauté on-ions and garlic until soft, about 5 minutes, adding small amounts of water, if needed, to prevent sticking.
2. Add remaining ingredients, except sour cream and herbs, and cook until tender, about 20 minutes.
3. Purée half of the soup in the blender and return to pot.
4. Serve soup hot or chilled with *Tofu Sour Cream* and herbs on top.

Tofu Sour Cream

makes 3/4 cup

5–6 ounces silken tofu, crumbled
2 Tbsp. *Cashew* or *Almond Cheese* (see pg. 22, 23)
1 Tbsp. lemon juice
1/2 tsp. brown rice syrup

1. Purée ingredients together until completely smooth.
2. Pour into a sprout bag or jar and allow to ferment for 8 to 12 hours. (See pg. 14 for information on fermenting.)

Beautifully colorful, with a gentle, sweet quality, this Russian favorite is one of my favorites! It's quick and easy to make and can be served hot or cold.

This simple non-dairy sour cream can be made easily if you have *Cashew* or *Almond Cheese,* or any nut cheese or yogurt on hand.

Guardian Angel, please help me always be open-minded.

A good way to use vegetable trimmings is to make a broth base for soups or sauces, or as a substitute for oil when sautéeing vegetables. The fragrance of simmering vegetable broth is always so comforting! The addition of herbs to this broth recipe makes it perfect for gravies and more complex soups.

*Guardian Angel,
please help me
remain in a state
of gratitude.*

Vegetable Herb Broth

makes 1 1/2 quarts

1 onion, peeled and quartered
2 cloves garlic, peeled and quartered
1 bunch parsley, including stems
2 stalks celery with leaves, sliced
1 carrot, sliced
1/4 head cabbage
1 bouquet garni or 1 bay leaf
3–4 dried mushrooms (porcine, crimini, or shiitake),
    soaked in 2 cups purified water
reserved mushroom soaking water
2 quarts purified water

1. Put all ingredients together in a large soup pot and bring to a boil. Reduce heat to simmer, cover, and allow to cook for one hour.
2. Strain vegetables from broth and discard. Store broth in an airtight container in the refrigerator for use in soups, gravies, and sauces.

Insights: Dried mushrooms often harbor dirt and sand, which will usually fall to the bottom of the bowl while soaking. After soaking, carefully remove each mushroom, rinse, and visually inspect. Strain the sand from the soaking liquid through a fine mess strainer. Never throw the soaking liquid away—add it to soups, sauces, gravies, and dressings.

Shiitake Vegetable Broth

makes 1 1/2 quarts

1 onion, peeled and quartered
2 cloves garlic, peeled and quartered
1 bunch parsley, including stems
2 stalks celery with leaves, sliced
6 dried shiitake mushrooms
2 quarts water

1. Combine all ingredients together in a heavy pot and bring to a boil. Reduce to simmer and cook for one hour.
2. Strain vegetables from broth and discard. Store broth in an airtight container in the refrigerator for use in soups, gravies, and sauces. Will keep for up to one week.

Shiitake Dashi

(Japanese Mushroom Broth)

makes 3 cups

6 large dried shiitake mushrooms
1 carrot, quartered
2-inch piece dried kombu seaweed
2 Tbsp. tamari soy sauce
1 tsp. Aji Mirin® sweet cooking rice wine

1. Combine ingredients with 1 quart of water and simmer, covered, for one hour.
2. Strain vegetables from broth and retain for use elsewhere, if desired.
3. Store broth in refrigerator and use as needed.

Shiitake mushrooms add a delicate smokiness to both of these soup broths. This delicate Japanese broth is used as a delicious base for Oriental soups and noodle dishes.

Guardian Angel, please help me to allow others to create their reality, as I create my own.

Chapter Eight

Gracious Grains

A Talk with Spirit about Choice

Celestial Guardians, please assist me in creating a life of health, joy, peace, and abundance. I ask for help in making choices based on my best interests and also on the best interests of all concerned. Help me respect the rights of others and accept my own right to choose in all things affecting my being. Assist me in recognizing that we are all fruits of the vine, ripening at our own rate of speed. I choose to lead a peaceful and harmonious life, filled with love and prosperity. I know that it is my birthright to have freedom of choice, and I ask for your Divine assistance in making the best choices possible.

I honor the Divinity in this food and in all life, and recognize that everything is an expression of the Love of God. As we blend our vibrations, our common love is multiplied. I love you, I bless you, I am one with you and the Divine Source of All That Is.

Recipes at a Glance

Gracious Grains

Naturally sweet and healthy, these sprouted cereals are hearty enough to hold you through the morning. Adding sprouted grains to cooked oatmeal increases the enzyme content as well as providing a nice texture.

Guardian Angel, please help me know that I am assisted in all things by Divine Guidance.

Sprouted Breakfast Cereal

makes 4–5 cups

1/2 cup soft wheat, kamut, or triticale
1/2 cup rye
1/2 cup buckwheat groats
1/2 cup sunflower seeds
sweetener of choice
ground cinnamon to taste
warm purified water or *Almond Milk* (see pg. 16)

1. Combine grains and seeds and soak in water overnight. Allow to sprout for 24 to 36 hours.(See pg. 7–9, *The Joys of Sprouting*)
2. Serve raw with warm or cold *Almond Milk* or water, cinnamon and sweetener. Remaining cereal can be stored in a refrigerator for up to 3 days.

Enlightened Oatmeal

serves 2

1 cup *Sprouted Breakfast Cereal* (see recipe above)
2 cups cooked oatmeal
1 cup warm purified water
1 cup *Almond* or *Cashew Yogurt* (see pg. 20)

1. Cook oatmeal and allow to cool to no more than 118 degrees (warm to the touch).
2. Combine grains and oatmeal in a blender and purée, adding small amounts of warm water, as needed, to keep the blender moving.
3. If possible, allow to sit in a warm place for 1/2 hour before eating.
4. Serve with *Almond* or *Cashew Yogurt* and sweetener.

Sprouted Grain Banana Blend

serves 1

1/2 cup sprouted buckwheat groats (see pg. 9)
1/4 cup sprouted wheat, kamut, or rye (see pg. 9)
1/2 Tbsp. flax seed
1/4 cup soaked almonds (see pg. 8) or
    sprouted sunflower seeds (see pg. 8)
1 banana, peeled
1 cup warm purified water

1. Combine ingredients in a blender and purée, adding as much water as needed to keep the blender moving. Enjoy!

Creamy Apple Grain Blend

serves 1

3/4 cup sprouted buckwheat groats (see pg. 9)
1/4 cup soaked almonds (see pg. 8)
1 apple, cored and quartered
2 tsp. Sucanat® (dehydrated sugar cane juice)
1/2 tsp. vanilla extract
1 cup warm purified water

1. Combine ingredients in a blender and purée, adding as much water as needed to keep the blender moving. Enjoy!

A quick and easy way to get your grains, these great blended drinks may be all you need to keep you going until lunchtime.

*Guardian Angel,
please help me
embrace the qualities
of love and kindness
that you possess.*

The ancient Essenes "cooked" their yeast-free, sprouted grain breads on sun-heated rocks in the desert. I imagine that Jesus, the most famous of the Essenes, ate bread very similar to this.

Guardian Angel,
please help me know
that I am greatly
loved by you
and other Entities
of Light and Love.

Multi-Grain Essene Bread

makes 2 small loaves

1/2 cup winter wheat berries or kamut
1/2 cup soft wheat berries
1/2 cup triticale
1/2 cup whole rye
1/4 cup millet
2 Tbsp. flax seeds
1/2 tsp. sea salt

1. Combine grains and seeds and soak in a 2-quart container for 24 hours. Drain, rinse, and drain again. Allow to sprout for another 24 hours, rinsing in 12 hours and again at the end of the 24-hour sprouting cycle. (See pg. 8, *The Joys of Sprouting.*)
2. Place well-rinsed grain in a food processor and roughly grind, using the "S" blade. The grains should begin to form a dough, but not be too finely ground. If using a Champion Juicer® use the blank filter and homogenize 1/2 of the grain. Fold the remaining grain into the batter before forming loaves. (The food processor makes a superior sprouted bread.)
3. Form 2 oval-shaped loaves, about 1–2 inches thick.
4. Place loaves on an oiled cookie sheet and bake in a vented, preheated 115-125 degree oven or food dehydrator for 3 hours. Turn over and "cook" another 4 to 6 hours or over night. Serve warm or store in refrigerator until ready to use. Will keep up to one week refrigerated.

Sprouted Rye Essene Rolls

makes 8–12 rolls

2 cups whole rye
2 Tbsp. flax seeds
1 tsp. caraway seeds
2 tsp. Braggs Liquid Aminos®
1/2 tsp. sea salt

1. Combine rye and seeds and soak in a 2-quart container for 24 hours. Drain, rinse, and drain again. Allow to sprout for another 24 hours, rinsing in 12 hours and again at the end of the 24-hour sprouting cycle. (See pg. 8, *The Joys of Sprouting.*)
2. Toss rye/seed mixture with Braggs, place in a food processor, and roughly grind using the "S" blade. The grains should begin to form a dough, but not be too finely ground. If using a Champion Juicer®, use the blank filter and homogenize 1/2 of the grain. Fold the remaining grain into the batter before shaping rolls. (The food processor makes superior sprouted rolls.)
3. Form 8 to 12 round or oblong shaped rolls, about 1- to 2-inches thick.
4. Place rolls on an oiled cookie sheet and bake in a vented, preheated 115-125 degree oven or food dehydrator for 3 hours. Turn over and "cook" another 4 to 6 hours. Serve warm or store in refrigerator until ready to use. Will keep up to one week refrigerated.

If you are sensitive to grains, you may find, as others have, that this uncooked, sprouted rye bread can be enjoyed without after effects. Always start with small tastes of new foods to test your reaction.

Guardian Angel, please help me see that all of us have our own paths and it's not for me to judge others.

Aromatic and flavorful, these bread sticks are delicious alone or with any of the *Sinful Spreads* (see pg. 53). If you don't have any *Seasoned Sunflower Seeds* on hand, simply use raw seeds of any kind and add your favorite seasonings.

*Guardian Angel,
please help me
always show respect
for myself and others.*

Savory Sunflower Bread Stix

makes 1–1 1/2 dozen bread sticks

1 cup wheat berries or kamut
1 cup whole rye
1/2 cup *Seasoned Sunflower Seeds* (see pg. 65)
1/2 tsp. sea salt

1. Combine grains and seeds and soak in a 2-quart container for 24 hours. Drain, rinse, and drain again. Allow to sprout for another 24 hours, rinsing in 12 hours and again at the end of the 24-hour sprouting cycle. (See pg. 8, *The Joys of Sprouting.*)

2. Place well-rinsed grain and seeds in a food processor and roughly grind, using the "S" blade. The grains should form a sticky dough. If using a Champion Juicer®, use the blank filter and homogenize 3/4 of the grain and seeds together. Fold the remaining grain and seeds into the batter before forming the bread sticks.

3. Divide dough into fourths. Using your palms roll each section of dough into long ropes, 3/4-inch thick and 5- to 6-inches long.

4. Place bread sticks on an oiled cookie sheet and bake in a vented, preheated 115-125 degree oven or food dehydrator for 3 hours. Turn over and "cook" another 4 to 6 hours. Serve warm or store in refrigerator until ready to use. Will keep up to one week refrigerated.

Glazed Molasses-Cinnamon Pinwheels

makes 8 pinwheels

2 cups wheat berries or kamut
1/4 cup black strap molasses
1 1/2 tsp. cinnamon
3 Tbsp. Sucanat® (dehydrated sugar cane juice)

1. Soak wheat berries in a 2-quart container for 24 hours. Drain, rinse, and drain again. Allow to sprout for 24 hours, rinsing in 12 hours and again at the end of the 24 hour sprouting cycle. (see pg. 8, *The Joys of Sprouting*)
2. Place well-rinsed grain in a bowl and mix in remaining ingredients, except Sucanat®. Place in a food processor and roughly grind using the "S" blade. The grains should form a sticky dough, but not be too finely ground. If using a Champion Juicer®, use the blank filter and homogenize 3/4 of the grain. Fold the remaining grain into the batter before forming pinwheels.
3. Divide dough into 8 portions. Using your palms roll each section of dough into long ropes, 3/4-inch thick, then shape each to form a spiral.
4. Place pinwheels on an oiled cookie sheet and bake in a vented, preheated 115-125 degree oven or food dehydrator for 3 hours. Turn over and "cook" another 4 to 6 hours.
5. Put Sucanat® in a clean nut or spice grinder and grind to a powder. Remove to a small bowl and moisten with a few drops of water at a time to form a thick glaze. Drizzle the glaze evenly over the pinwheels prior to serving. Serve warm, or store in refrigerator until ready to use.

Naturally sweet and wholesome, these sprouted, uncooked cinnamon rolls or pinwheels are simple to make compared to other sweet breads and can easily be varied to suit your taste.

Guardian Angel, please help me know that I can be who I really am without losing love.

Luscious dates and rich walnuts add complexity and texture to these scones. For a special treat serve them with some *Sweetened Cashew Cheese* or *Sweet Almond Spread.* (See pg. 26, 68.)

Guardian Angel,
please help me
know God and
see God in everyone
and everything.

Date-Walnut Scones

makes 8 scones

1 cup wheat berries or kamut
1 cup whole rye
12–20 pitted dates (depending on size and sweetness)
1 cup walnut pieces
1 tsp. cinnamon
1/8 tsp. nutmeg

1. Combine wheat and rye and soak in a 2–quart container for 24 hours. Drain, rinse, and drain again. Allow grains to sprout for 24 hours, rinsing in 12 hours and again at the end of the 24-hour sprouting cycle. (See pg. 8, *The Joys of Sprouting.*)
2. Place well-rinsed grain in a bowl and mix in remaining ingredients. Place in a food processor and roughly grind using the "S" blade. The grains should begin to form a dough, but not be too finely ground. If using a Champion Juicer®, use the blank filter and homogenize 1/2 of the grain. Fold the remaining grain into the batter before forming scones. (The food processor makes superior sprouted scones.)
3. Firmly press dough into a round cake pan and cut 8 equal pie-shaped slices.
4. Carefully remove each slice and place them on an oiled cookie sheet and bake in a vented, preheated 115-125 degree oven or food dehydrator for 3 hours. Turn over and "cook" another 4 to 6 hours. Serve warm, or store in refrigerator until ready to use. Will keep up to one week refrigerated.

Sprouted Grain Crisps

makes 4 dozen

2 cups mixed grain sprouts (see pg. 8)
1 tsp. nutritional yeast
dash of onion powder
dash of garlic powder
1 tsp. Vege-Sal® or Braggs Liquid Aminos® to taste
10–12 ounces water
1/4 cup sesame seeds or poppy seeds

1. Combine ingredients, except seeds, in a blender and purée.
2. Drop by the tablespoon onto dehydrator sheets and shake to flatten, forming silver dollar-size rounds.
3. Sprinkle with sesame seeds or poppy seeds and allow to dehydrate until crisp, about 12 to 24 hours.
4. Store covered, in a cool, dark place.

Sea Vegetable Grain Crisps

makes 4 dozen

2 cups mixed grain sprouts (see pg. 8)
1 tsp. nutritional yeast
dash of garlic powder
1/2 tsp. tamari soy sauce
1 tsp. ground dulse, kelp, or nori
10–12 ounces water
1/4 cup sesame seeds

1. Combine ingredients, except seeds, in a blender and purée.
2. Drop by the tablespoon onto dehydrator sheets and shake to flatten, forming silver-dollar size rounds.
3. Sprinkle with sesame seeds and allow to dehydrate until crisp, about 12 to 24 hours.
4. Store, covered, in a cool, dark place.

It's hard to believe that these crackers are uncooked! They are thin and crispy and can be served as you would serve any other cracker. Vary the seasoning to suit your mood. I love seaweed and use it to season everything from popcorn to soup! It's full of trace minerals and other illusive nutrients.

*Guardian Angel,
please help me
base all my decisions on
Love and Trust.*

Aromatic herbs add to the already heavenly smell of this bread when it's baking. There's nothing more homey and comforting than freshly baked bread!

Guardian Angel,
please help me
let go of fear
and be free!

Fragrant Onion Herb Rolls

makes 12 rolls

1 Tbsp. dry active yeast
1 Tbsp. brown rice syrup
1 cup warm water

1 1/2 cups whole wheat flour

1 medium onion, minced
1/2 tsp. olive oil
1 clove garlic, minced
1/2 tsp. crushed basil
1/2 tsp. crushed marjoram
1/2 tsp. crushed summer savory
1/4 tsp. crushed rosemary

1 Tbsp. olive oil
1/2 tsp. sea salt
1 1/2 cups unbleached flour

1 Tbsp. cornmeal
olive oil cooking spray

1. Dissolve the yeast and syrup in warm water and allow to work for 5 to 10 minutes.
2. To form a sponge, stir in the whole wheat flour using no less than 100 strokes. Cover and allow to rise in a warm place for 20 minutes.
3. Meanwhile, heat a skillet to medium and add 1/2 tsp. oil. Sauté onions until soft and transparent, about 5 minutes. Remove from heat and mix in garlic and herbs.

4. Pour 1 tablespoon of oil and salt over the sponge and fold it in. (Be careful not to break the sponge into pieces.)
5. Begin kneading the unbleached flour into the sponge using 1/4 cup at a time, until you have used 3/4 cup.
6. Pour the onion mixture over the dough and gently knead it in, slowly adding the remaining 1/2 cup flour to keep it from sticking to the board.
7. Place the dough in an oiled bowl, cover with a damp towel and allow it to rest in a warm place for 1 hour.
8. Punch the dough down to its original size and roll into a 1 1/2 - to 2-inch cylinder. Slice into 12 equal pieces.
9. Place rolls on a cornmeal-dusted baking sheet and spray them with oil. Allow to rise in a warm place for 15 to 20 minutes.
10. Meanwhile, preheat oven to 375 degrees.
11. Bake rolls in preheated oven for 20 minutes, or until golden brown.

Insights: Active dry yeast does not live forever, so keep it in an airtight container in the refrigerator and, to be safe, replace it every 6 months. To use, remove your measure of yeast and allow it to come to room temperature before adding it to warm water. Make certain the water is only warm to the touch, not hot. Stir once, then do not disturb the yeast while it's growing, which will take from 5 to 10 minutes. If it's not full and frothy at that time, the yeast may not be active. Rather than taking the chance of ruining your bread, throw it away and start again with fresh yeast.

For a really delightful non-dairy spread, try the *French Oven-Roasted Garlic* or *Roasted Garlic Cheese Spread.* (See pg. 61, 73.)

Guardian Angel, please help me remember who I really am and why I am here.

Easy to make and hard to beat, these corn muffins are wonderful and naturally sweet. As with all quick breads, don't beat them up—just gently stir the batter until all the dry ingredients are moist. Feel free to add fresh corn, minced peppers, or anything else that pleases you!

Guardian Angel,
please help me
evolve into the essence
of angelic grace and
Love.

Unbeatable Corn Muffins

serves 4

1 3/4 cups yellow cornmeal
3/4 cup whole wheat flour
2 Tbsp. vegan powdered egg replacer (Ener-G® brand)
2 tsp. baking powder
1/2 tsp. baking soda
1 tsp. sea salt

1 1/4 cups plain soy milk, rice milk, or nut milk
1 1/2 Tbsp. corn oil
1/4 cup maple syrup

1. Preheat oven to 375 degrees.
2. Oil muffin pans.
3. Combine and sift dry ingredients together. Set aside.
4. Mix liquid ingredients together.
5. Pour liquid ingredients into cornmeal mixture and stir until just blended. (Do not beat.)
6. Pour into an oiled muffin pan and bake in preheated oven for 20 minutes. Serve warm.

Tabouli
(Middle Eastern Sprouted Wheat with Parsley)

serves 4

1 cup very young wheat or kamut sprouts (see pg. 9)
2 green onions, finely sliced
2 cups parsley, minced
1/4 cup fresh mint, minced (optional)
1 medium-size ripe tomato, seeded and diced
1/4 cup lemon juice
2 Tbsp. flax oil or extra-virgin olive oil
1 tsp. sea salt (or, to taste)
freshly ground pepper (to taste)

1. Pulse-grind wheat in a food processor until each kernel is broken into 2 or more pieces. Do not overly process—the grains should only be broken.
2. Add green onions, parsley, and mint, and briefly process again.
3. In another bowl, combine remaining ingredients and stir.
4. Mix all ingredients together thoroughly by hand.
5. Serve chilled or gently heated. Will keep up to two days refrigerated.

Often served as a salad, this sprouted grain version of the traditional Tabouli is far more nutritious and digestible than its counterpart. Seasonings can be varied to create unfired pilafs of different kinds. Enjoy it chilled, or gently warm it.

*Guardian Angel,
please help me
make decisions based
on Truth and Light.*

Polenta is a staple of the Mediterranean region. I especially like this version, which is smothered with mushrooms! It's also delicious with *Sweet Red Pepper Sauce* or *Fresh Marinara Sauce.* (See pg. 162, 158.)

Guardian Angel, please help me remain peaceful and serene even when challenged.

Polenta
(Italian-Style Cornmeal)
with Grilled Mushrooms
serves 4

3 cups purified water (divided use)
1/2 cup onions, minced
2 cloves garlic, minced
1 small carrot, minced
1/2 cup red bell pepper, minced
2 Tbsp. chopped fresh basil leaves
2 Tbsp. chopped parsley
1/2 tsp. sea salt
freshly ground pepper
1 cup coarsely-ground cornmeal (see following *Insight*)
olive oil cooking spray
1 recipe *Grilled Mushrooms* (see following recipe)

1. Heat large saucepan with 1/4 cup of water. Sauté onions and garlic in the water for 5 minutes, adding more water if needed to prevent sticking.
2. Add carrots and red peppers and cook 2 more minutes. Stir in basil, parsley, water, salt, and pepper and bring to a boil.
3. Add cornmeal in a slow steady stream, stirring constantly.
4. Reduce heat to simmer and cook uncovered for 20 minutes, stirring frequently. When a wooden spoon placed in the center of the cooked polenta can stand up on its own, it's ready.
5. Wet a clean, large cutting board or formica workspace with water, and spread the polenta out in a square or rectangle, about 1/2-inch thick. Allow it to cool and become firm.
6. Slice the polenta into 3-inch triangles, spray with olive oil, and grill or broil until golden brown on both sides.
7. Serve hot, topped with *Grilled Mushrooms.*

Grilled Mushrooms

serves 4

olive oil cooking spray or 1 tsp. olive oil
1 pound mushrooms, washed, dried, and sliced
2 cloves garlic, minced
2 Tbsp. chopped parsley
sea salt
freshly ground pepper

1. Heat skillet or grill to medium-hot and season with oil. Sauté mushrooms and garlic until mushrooms are golden brown, adding additional water, as needed, to prevent sticking.
2. Add parsley, cover and reduce heat to low until ready to serve. If necessary, add a few more tablespoons of water to prevent sticking.
3. Season to taste with salt and pepper, and serve over *Grilled Polenta* (see opposite page) or *Caribbean Cornmeal with Okra* (see pg. 152).

Insights: Polenta is a coarsely ground cornmeal that can be cooked like grits or porridge, or cooled and cut into shapes. It's used widely in Italian cuisine, in place of pasta, and in some Caribbean and Southern cooking. Polenta is easy to prepare, but requires almost constant stirring to keep it from burning as it thickens. The amount of water used will determine its consistency. When polenta cools, it becomes thicker and will even become firm, allowing for a variety of shapes to be created. Cut it into squares, triangles, or use cookie cutters to create other fun shapes.

Mushrooms and garlic unite in this intensely flavorful topping that can enhance everything from rice and polenta to toast and pasta. Try various types of mushrooms such as chanterelles, morels, portobellos, shiitakes, or plain field mushrooms—they are all great!

Guardian Angel, please help me respect the uniqueness of others.

Lightly toasting grains make them fragrant and delicious, and keep a pilaf from getting mushy or sticky. This savory millet pilaf will delight your senses!

Wonderfully spicy and fragrant, *garam masala* is lovely added to grain dishes and curried vegetables.

*Guardian Angel,
please help me
live in harmony with
the earth.*

Middle Eastern
Millet Pilaf with Cashews
serves 4

1 cup millet
olive oil cooking spray or 1/2 tsp. olive oil
1/2 medium onion, minced
1 clove garlic, crushed
1/2 tsp. fresh ginger, peeled and minced
1/4–1/2 tsp. fresh green chili, seeded and minced
1/4 cup cashew pieces
1/2 tsp. *Garam Masala Seasoning* (see following recipe)
1/2 tsp. sea salt
1 3/4 cups purified water

1. Heat a dry non-stick skillet to medium and add millet. Toast millet, stirring, until it turns lightly golden, and set aside.
2. Heat a deep skillet to medium-hot and season with oil. Sauté onions for a few minutes, adding small amounts of water as needed to prevent sticking. Add garlic, ginger, and chili, and cook for another minute or two.
3. Add millet and remaining ingredients, and stir. Bring to a boil, cover, reduce to low heat, and simmer for 30 minutes. Remove from heat and allow to sit, covered, for 10 to 15 minutes before serving.

Garam Masala Seasoning

1 Tbsp. whole cardamom seeds
1 one-inch stick of cinnamon
1 tsp. each cumin seeds, whole cloves, and peppercorns
1/3 average-sized whole nutmeg

1. Grind ingredients together in a spice grinder until powdery.

East Indian Basmati Rice Pilaf

serves 4

olive oil cooking spray or 1/2 tsp. olive oil
1 tsp. black mustard seeds
1/2 medium onion, minced
2 cloves garlic, minced
1 tsp. fresh ginger, peeled and minced
1 cup basmati rice, rinsed well and drained
1 cup mushrooms, chopped
1 tsp. *Garam Masala Seasoning* (see opposite page)
1 tsp. ground coriander
1 Tbsp. fresh parsley, chopped
1/2 tsp. sea salt (or, to taste)
1 3/4 cup water

1. Heat non-stick skillet to medium-hot and season with oil. Add mustard seeds and cook until they begin to pop. Add onion to skillet and stir. Sauté onions until transparent, about 5 minutes, adding small amounts of water as needed to prevent sticking.
2. Add garlic and ginger, and continue cooking another minute.
3. Stir in rice, mushrooms, *Garam Masala,* and coriander; and cook about 10 minutes, stirring often.
4. Add water, parsley, and salt, and bring to a boil. Cover, reduce heat to low, and simmer for 25 minutes. Do not stir.
5. Remove from heat and allow to sit, covered, for 10 more minutes.

Basmati rice is wonderfully aromatic and flavorful even without the benefit of seasoning. This savory, seasoned pilaf is extraordinarily delectable!

Guardian Angel, please assist me in sending Light out to the planet and all who need it.

I first tasted cornmeal with okra in Barbados and couldn't wait to come home and make my own version. Corn and okra are both favorites in our house, so it was an instant winner!

Guardian Angel,
please help me
expand the Love
in my heart
and the Light
in my mind.

Caribbean Cornmeal with Okra

12 small whole okra, cut into 1/4-inch rounds
3 cups water
1/2 tsp. sea salt
1 Tbsp. powdered vegetarian "chicken-flavored" broth
2 tsp. fresh jalapeno pepper, seeded and minced
1 cup yellow corn meal
1/2 cup fresh or frozen (defrosted) corn kernels
1/4 red bell pepper, seeded and diced
2 green onions, sliced

1. Bring water and salt to a boil, and add okra. Reduce heat to simmer and cook for 5 minutes.
2. Add broth and jalapeno peppers and slowly stir in cornmeal. Continue cooking cornmeal, stirring for 5 to 10 minutes, until mixture becomes very thick.
3. Stir in remaining ingredients and pour into oiled mold or casserole dish.
4. Serve immediately or keep in warm oven until serving time.

Insights: Okra is an edible green pod that is available fresh during the summer months. It can be sliced and eaten raw, or sauteed, steamed, and added to soups. Okra contains a slippery juice that adds body to soups and is very soothing to the digestive tract. It's a delicious and unusual vegetable for adventurous spirits.

Wild Rice Almond Pilaf

serves 4

olive oil cooking spray or 1/2 tsp. olive oil
2 Tbsp. shallots, minced
1 cup long grain brown rice, washed and drained
1/2 cup shredded carrots
1 cup mushrooms, chopped
1/2 cup celery, sliced thin
2 cups fresh spinach or chard, rinsed well, drained, and
    finely chopped (or 1 cup frozen leaf spinach)
1 Tbsp. barley miso
1 Tbsp. powdered vegetarian "chicken-flavored" broth
1 tsp. ground marjoram
1 tsp. ground sage
4 cups boiling purified water (divided use)
1/2 cup wild rice, washed and drained
1/2 cup (2 ounces) slivered almonds, lightly toasted

1. Heat a heavy non-stick pot to medium and season with oil.
   Gently sauté shallots for couple of minutes, adding small
   amounts of water as needed to prevent sticking.
2. Add remaining ingredients, except wild rice, 2 cups water,
   and almonds, and bring to a boil. Reduce heat to simmer,
   cover tightly, and cook for 50 minutes. Do not stir. Turn off
   heat and allow to sit undisturbed for another 10 minutes.
3. While rice and vegetables are cooking, combine wild rice
   and 2 cups water in a saucepan and bring it to a boil. Cover
   loosely and reduce to a slow boil (medium heat). Cook for
   45 to 60 minutes or until tender. Drain well.
4. Gently fold in wild rice and almonds. Serve hot.

Holidays and celebrations call for something really special! In our house, this pilaf has become a family tradition at Thanksgiving and Christmas.

*Guardian Angel,
please help me
think the thoughts
that angels think.*

Mexican Seasoned Rice

serves 4

1 cup medium grain brown rice, rinsed and drained
olive oil cooking spray or 1/2 tsp. olive oil
1 clove garlic, minced
3 green onions, thinly sliced
1/2 tomato, peeled, seeded, and diced
1/4 cup tomato sauce
1 3/4 cups hot purified water
1 tsp. sea salt (or, to taste)
1/4 cup fresh or frozen peas

1. Heat a deep non-stick skillet or pot (one with a tight fitting lid) to medium-hot, and season with oil. Add rice, onions and garlic to skillet and cook for several minutes, stirring, until grains of rice become opaque and no longer stick together. (They will begin to show signs of being toasted.)
2. Combine water, tomato sauce, and salt, and add to rice.
3. Bring to a boil, then cover, and reduce heat. Simmer for 50 minutes without lifting the lid.
4. Remove lid, add peas, replace lid, and remove from heat. Allow to sit, without disturbing, for 10 minutes before serving.

Insights: If tomatoes are organically grown and will be prepared raw, the skins may be left on, but cooking will loosen the skins from tomatoes and separate, so removing the skin is preferred. To peel a tomato, you can do one of three things: scorch the skin under the broiler or over a gas flame for a few minutes, or drop it into boiling water for a couple of minutes (both of which will loosen the skin enough to easily peel off), or peel it using a sharp paring knife.

The secret to Mexican-style rice is toasting the grains. It keeps the tomatoes and seasonings from making the rice gummy, even when using brown rice. Gently toasting it first adds a nutty taste to the rice and keeps the dish fluffy and the kernels separated.

Guardian Angel,
please help me
let go of the past
and forgive.

Chinese Vegetable Fried Rice

serves 4

1 cup medium grain brown rice, washed and drained
1 3/4 cups water
4 ounces tofu, rinsed, drained, and mashed
1/4 tsp. turmeric
1/8 tsp. sea salt
3/4 cup cabbage, shredded
1/2 cup zucchini, julienned
1/4 bell pepper, julienned
1 medium carrot, julienned
4 green onions, sliced
6 medium-size mushrooms, chopped
1 1/2 tsp. sesame oil
1/2 tsp. Aji Mirin® (sweet rice wine)
1/4 tsp. brown rice syrup (or other sweetener)
1 Tbsp. tamari soy sauce

1. Combine rice and water in heavy pot or electric rice cooker. Bring to a boil, reduce heat to simmer, and allow to steam for 50 minutes without lifting lid. When rice has cooked and water is absorbed, remove from heat and allow to sit, without lifting lid, for another 10 to 15 minutes.
2. Remove lid from rice, and cool rice to room temperature.
3. Mash tofu with turmeric and salt. Stir well and set aside.
4. Heat wok or skillet to medium-hot and add 1/2 tsp. oil. When oil is hot, add rice and stir-fry for 2 minutes. Remove rice from wok and set aside.
5. Using the same wok, add another 1/2 tsp. oil and heat the tofu mixture. Stir-fry for one minute and remove.
6. Add the last 1/2 tsp. oil to wok and stir-fry the vegetables until almost cooked, about 1 to 3 minutes.
7. Mix rice wine, sweetener, and soy sauce, and add to wok.
8. Stir in rice and tofu, and cook until mixture is hot.

Fried rice is usually loaded with oil, and although it is delicious, it doesn't always leave you feeling good. This recipe is light and fulfilling without all the oil.

*Guardian Angel,
please help me
be sovereign
and self-determined.*

Chapter Nine

Miraculous Main Dishes

A Talk with Spirit about Peace of Mind

Angelic Presence, please help me cultivate inner peace so I may experience the world around me as a peaceful place. I desire to be centered in peacefulness. I ask that you help me hold peace as a central focus in my heart and mind, so that even when I am challenged, I remain calm and relaxed. I am thankful for your love, your assistance, and all the opportunities for growth that you provide for me. Help me trust in this process so I can be relaxed with it. Help me trust that everything is happening in Divine order, and allow it to bring joy and serenity into my life.

I am filled with gratitude for these precious gifts of nourishment, and I recognize them as symbols of the great abundance that is constantly provided by the Divine Source of All That Is. I love you, I bless you, I am one with you.

Recipes at a Glance

Italian-Style Living Lasagna

serves 4

This unusual raw lasagna is guaranteed to turn heads! You may roast the eggplant if you prefer. Simply double the amount called for in the recipe, slice thicker, and oven roast. For variety, use peeled, thinly sliced, raw zucchini instead of eggplant.

Guardian Angel, please help me know that I am a perfect child of God.

Fresh Marinara Sauce:
2 medium-size tomatoes, seeded and chopped
1 ounce (3/4 cup) sun-dried tomatoes, soaked for 2 hours and drained
1/8 cup fresh parsley leaves, minced
1 Tbsp. minced onion
4 large fresh basil leaves, minced
1/2 small clove garlic, crushed
1/2 tsp. dry oregano leaves, crushed
1/8 tsp. sea salt (or, to taste)
freshly ground pepper

1 cup *Almond Ricotta Cheese* (see pg. 28)
1/2 small eggplant, peeled, thinly sliced, and soaked in salted water to cover for 30 minutes
3 cups (packed) spinach leaves, washed, dried, and minced
8 medium-size mushrooms, cleaned and thinly sliced

1. Combine ingredients for *Sauce* in food processor and purée.
2. Line a 22" x 12" loaf pan with a large double layer of cheese-cloth, so that the cloth drapes over all sides of the pan.
3. To assemble, drain eggplant and pat dry. Place one layer of eggplant on top of the cheesecloth at the bottom of the loaf pan. Evenly spread 1/3 of the *Marinara Sauce* on top.
4. Place 1/2 of the sliced mushrooms evenly over the sauce and spread 1/2 of the *Almond Ricotta Cheese* on top.
5. Evenly distribute 1/2 of the ground spinach over the top of the *Almond Ricotta Cheese* and press firmly into place.
6. Repeat steps 3–5 using 1/2 of the *Marinara* and all of the remaining ingredients—layering them on top of the first layer.
7. Cover the top with the remaining *Marinara Sauce*.
8. Lifting the cheesecloth, carefully remove lasagna, and slice into 4 pieces. Serve at room temperature or gently heated.

Mediterranean Harvest Casserole

serves 6–8

2 large eggplants, peeled and sliced 1/2-inch thick
1 qt. water and 2 Tbsp. salt
1 1/3 cup *Almond Cheese* (see pg. 22)
2 Tbsp. finely minced fresh basil
4 cups packed fresh greens (spinach or sunflower greens),
    washed, dried, and minced
12 medium-size fresh mushrooms, cleaned and diced
2 fresh bell peppers, seeded and diced
4 medium-size ripe tomatoes, seeded and diced
1/4 cup leeks (or red onion), diced
dash of garlic powder
1/2 tsp. Braggs Liquid Aminos® (or sea salt, to taste)

1. Soak eggplant slices in salted water to cover for 30 minutes.
   Remove, rinse, and pat dry.
2. Preheat oven to 400 degrees. Lay eggplant on a broiler tray
   and roast for 10 to 15 minutes. Remove and chop.
3. Line an 8 x 8 x 2-inch square glass baking dish evenly with
   half of the eggplant.
4. Combine cheese, basil, and greens and mix well.
5. Spread half of cheese mixture evenly on top of eggplant.
6. Layer mushrooms and bell peppers on top of cheese mixture
   and press firmly. Spread remaining cheese on top.
7. Layer remaining eggplant evenly on top of cheese mixture.
8. Mix tomatoes, leeks, garlic powder, and Braggs®, and spread
   uniformly over the top.
9. Serve at room temperature or gently heated in oven.

Unique and delicious, this recipe is one of our favorites! I recommend roasting the eggplant, but if you prefer it can be prepared 100% raw. Simply reduce the amount of eggplant in the recipe to one eggplant, shredded.

Guardian Angel, please help me open up and shine my Light on others.

Everyone loves pasta, but cooked wheat pasta may not agree with everyone's digestion. We find that shredded zucchini is a great substitute to hold all those wonderful pasta sauces. It can be eaten chilled as a salad, or gently warmed, which softens it to an al dente texture.

Guardian Angel,
please help me
share my guidance,
love, and wisdom.

Italian-Style Zucchini Pasta Pesto

serves 4

2 medium zucchini, julienned or shredded lengthwise to resemble pasta (see *Insights* below)
8–10 mushrooms, chopped
2–3 Tbsp. *Pesto* (see pg. 70)
1/4 cup water
4–6 sun-dried tomatoes, soaked until soft, then julienned

1. Toss all ingredients together, except the tomatoes.
2. Serve chilled on a bed of greens and garnished with tomatoes, or gently warm it in the oven to soften the zucchini and garnish with tomatoes prior to serving.

Insights: To make zucchini resemble pasta, use a food processor with a julienne attachment, or a hand shredder, and shred lengthwise to create long, fine, linguine-like strands. Warm it gently, and it will soften to the texture of al dente pasta.

Italian Zucchini Pasta with Spinach

serves 4

Sauce:
1/2 clove garlic, crushed
1 Tbsp. flax oil or extra-virgin olive oil
1 Tbsp. minced fresh basil
1 Tbsp. lime juice or balsamic vinegar
freshly ground pepper

2–3 medium zucchini, julienned or shredded lengthwise
　to resemble pasta (see opposite *Insights*)
2 large ripe tomatoes, seeded and diced
10 Greek olives
2 cups (packed) spinach, washed, dried, and chopped

1. Combine ingredients for sauce and set aside.
2. Gently toss remaining ingredients together.
3. Pour sauce over vegetables and toss again. Serve at room temperature or gently heated.

Insights: Balsamic vinegars vary greatly in flavor due to aging methods and you'll see this reflected in store prices. This type of vinegar is very brown in color (which makes it unsuitable for potato salad and other dishes that are light in color) and is sweeter and milder than most other types of vinegars. Use Balsamic vinegar in marinades, salad dressings, and sauces, or anytime a sweet-and-sour flavor is desired.

This is a great use for some of the zucchini from your garden! Yellow squash, sweet potatoes, or yams shredded "angel-hair" thin also makes great pasta. We prefer it gently warmed, which softens it to an al dente texture, but don't overheat it if you want to protect those delicate enzymes!

*Guardian Angel,
I look to you
with faith that I will
become like you
in spirit.*

Angelic cuisine at it's finest! This recipe will delight even your most skeptical friends and win them over to fresh, uncooked foods. Combined with the *Sweet Red Pepper Sauce*, it is heavenly!

Guardian Angel,
I look to you
with faith that
I will always
know Love.

Zucchini Onion Croquettes with Sweet Red Pepper Sauce

serves 4

4 small zucchini, shredded
1/2 cup *Cashew Cream Cheese* (see pg. 23)
2 Tbsp. toasted dehydrated onions
2 tsp. Onion Magic® or other onion seasoning
1/2 tsp. unpasteurized light miso paste
1/2 tsp. nutritional yeast
dash of nutmeg and white pepper

1. Combine ingredients and mix well, using your hands.
2. Form 8 small oval-shaped patties about 1/2-inch thick.
3. Place on plastic sheets in a dehydrator no hotter than 118 degrees for 2 to 4 hours. (An oven that has been warmed at the lowest temperature setting and turned off may be used in place of a dehydrator. Periodically remove the croquettes to reheat the oven, then turn the oven off before returning the croquettes to the warm oven.)
4. Serve slightly warm with *Sweet Red Pepper Sauce*.

Sweet Red Pepper Sauce

makes 1 1/2 cup

1 red bell pepper, seeded and chopped
1/2 cup *Cashew Cream Cheese* (see pg. 23)
2 Tbsp. red onion, minced
1 Tbsp. lemon juice
1/2 Tbsp. light miso
1 tsp. dill weed
dash of white pepper

1. Combine ingredients in a blender and purée until smooth.

Mexican Bean Sprout & Vegetable Burritos

serves 4 (8 burritos)

3 cups greens (sunflower, lettuce, spinach, etc.), chopped
2 long green (Anaheim) chilies or 1 small green bell
   pepper, seeded and diced
1 small zucchini, washed and diced
2 medium-size tomatoes, seeded and diced
3/4 cup mixed young bean sprouts (see pg. 9)
2 green onions, sliced
2 Tbsp. minced fresh cilantro
1/2 cup *Seasoned Almond* or *Cashew Cheese* (see pg. 26)
1/2 tsp. Braggs Liquid Aminos® (or sea salt, to taste)
dash hot sauce (optional)
8 spelt or whole wheat tortillas (or large cabbage or
   lettuce leaves)

1. Combine all ingredients, except tortillas, and toss well.
2. Heat tortillas individually over stove top grill or in a cast iron pan, putting them between two clean dish towels to keep them warm.
3. Meanwhile warm filling ingredients slightly on low heat.
4. Place filling along the center of the tortillas, allowing a 2-inch space at one end. Fold that end in toward the center and roll the two sides over the filling to form a long roll. Serve immediately.

This is a bean burrito that won't have you hiding in the bathroom! Sprouted beans are far more digestible than their cooked counterparts and are still high in protein and fiber. We love this burrito as is, but you may wish to serve it with *Mexican Tomato Salsa* (see pg. 54).

Guardian Angel, please assist me in recognizing the abundant help and inspiration available to me.

Like many people, we love Vietnamese food, especially these *Vietnamese Salad Rolls* because they aren't deep fried and they are incredibly delicious! This recipe requires a little practice to master the rolling technique, but once you've done it, you'll want to do it again and again!

*Guardian Angel,
please help me
know that your Love
enfolds me and
keeps me safe.*

Vietnamese Salad Rolls

serves 4–6

2 recipes very thick *Bon Bon Sauce* (see pg. 169)
1/2–1 tsp. Thai red curry paste or 1/8 tsp. cayenne pepper
12 medium-size sheets Banh-Trang (special wheat or rice spring roll wrappers, available through Asian markets)
1 bunch spinach (leaves only) or green-leaf lettuce, thoroughly washed and dried
3 cups Asian-style bean sprouts
2–3 carrots, shredded
2 green onions, sliced
1 bunch cilantro (Chinese parsley) or 12 large basil leaves, washed and dried

1. Prepare work area by having all ingredients within easy reach. Make sure you have a bowl of clean water and a clear work surface.
2. Combine *Bon Bon Sauce* with curry to suit your taste.
3. Immerse two wrappers in water for a minute to soften.
4. Divide your spinach leaves into 12 equal portions, layering each group of leaves (no more than 4–5) evenly, one on top of the other.
5. Lay one wrapper down on your work surface and place the second wrapper on top, about one quarter of the way down, so that they overlap. (This reinforces the central area with two layers and provides a longer rolling surface.)

6. Stack one group of spinach about a quarter of the way up from the edge closest to you, leaving at least 1 to 2 inches free on each side.
7. Place 1 Tbsp. of *Bon Bon-Curry* mixture evenly on top of the spinach.
8. Place 1/4 cup of bean sprouts, some shredded carrot, and a few slices of green onions evenly on top.
9. Cover with a few sprigs of cilantro.
10. Fold the wrapper to cover the filling and pull gently back to pack the mixture firmly together. Begin rolling toward the end, tucking sides in before the cylindrical roll is completed.
11. Repeat steps 3–10 until all rolls are prepared.
12. Serve at room temperature, with a little extra *Bon Bon - Curry* for dipping.

Insights: Cilantro, also known as Chinese parsley, is actually the leaf of the coriander plant. It's used widely in Mexican, Chinese, East Indian, and Moroccan dishes. Overcooking destroys the flavor of this delicate leaf, so add it toward the end of cooking time, or use as a garnish. The stems are great added to fresh vegetable juice or soup broths. Coriander seeds and leaves are not interchangeable in recipes.

There are many brands of Thai curry paste, but most contain fish extract, so read the ingredients carefully if you wish to avoid animal products. I like Thai Kitchen® brand red curry paste.

Guardian Angel, please illuminate my soul path and keep me on track.

Sushi rolls are fun to make and even more fun to eat! Even children love sushi! The varieties are limited only by imagination. Here are a few samples of our favorite sushi recipes. (Directions follow recipes.)

*Guardian Angel,
please help me
exemplify the essence
of spiritual integrity.*

Japanese Sushimaki
(Vegetables Rolled in Seaweed)

Vegemaki

makes 2 vegetable rolls

2 tsp. dark miso or *Spicy Paste* (see next page)
2 cups alfalfa sprouts or sunflower greens
1/2 carrot, shredded
1/4 cucumber or zucchini, cut lengthwise julienne-style
1/2 red bell pepper, seeded and cut julienne-style
2 sheets of untoasted of musubi-nori (seaweed)

Spicy Avocado-Cucumber Maki

makes 2 avocado-cucumber rolls

2 tsp. *Spicy Paste* (see next page)
1 1/2–2 cups alfalfa sprouts
1/2 cucumber, cut lengthwise julienne-style
1/2 avocado, peeled and sliced into 6 slices
sesame seeds in shaker
2 sheets of untoasted of musubi-nori (seaweed)

Thai-Style Maki

makes 2 rolls

2 tsp. *Spicy Paste* (see next page)
2 leaves green-leaf lettuce, washed and dried thoroughly
1/4 cup bean sprouts
2 Tbsp. peanuts, minced
4 large sprigs cilantro (Chinese parsley)
2 sheets of untoasted musubi-nori (seaweed)

California Rice & Avocado Maki

makes 2 rolls

2 tsp. unpasteurized dark miso or *Spicy Paste*
1 cup cooked medium or short grain brown rice
1/2 cucumber, cut lengthwise julienne-style
1/2 avocado, peeled and sliced into 6 slices
sesame seeds in shaker
2 sheets of untoasted of musubi-nori (seaweed)

Japanese Spicy Paste:
2 Tbsp. unpasteurized dark miso paste
1/2 tsp. ground fresh chili paste (Sambal Olek®)
1/4 tsp. toasted sesame oil

pickled ginger root or onion sprouts
tamari soy sauce or Braggs®

General Directions for Above Recipes:

1. Put all ingredients and necessary equipment near you on the counter before rolling sushimaki.
2. Place a sheet of nori on a bamboo sushi mat or dish cloth.
3. Using 1 teaspoon of *Spicy Paste* or miso, draw a line horizontally, 2/3 of the way down, through the center of the nori.
4. Lay 1/2 of the prepared vegetables for each type of maki on top of the paste, beginning with the lettuce or alfalfa, then the bean sprouts or rice, followed by the rest, allowing a little to extend beyond the side ends of the nori wrapper.
5. Use the bamboo mat or cloth to help roll *Maki* jelly-roll style. When the roll is complete, press down gently on the mat beginning at the center and working out to the sides to ensure correct firmness.
6. Remove to a cutting board and slice into 8 equal pieces. Roll remaining *maki*, one at a time, following steps 2–6.
7. Separate rolls and arrange attractively on a tray. Serve with soy sauce or Braggs® and pickled ginger or onion sprouts.

Nori is the most widely used of all the ocean-grown vegetables. It's formed into large, paper-thin, flat sheets and is available toasted or raw. I prefer the untoasted variety because of the higher enzyme content. All sea vegetables are high in trace minerals and many contain vitamin B_{12}.

Guardian Angel,
please help me
accept change and
evolve into
all that I can be.

This colorful nest of shredded vegetables is as pretty as it is delicious! As with many Thai recipes, this one calls for coconut milk, but nut milk or even rice milk will work. You may also substitute any fresh, finely julienned vegetable that you prefer.

Guardian Angel, please help me maintain a course of spiritual growth and enlightenment.

Thai Crane's Nest in Coconut Curry

serves 4

1 cup coconut milk
1 tsp. Thai red curry paste
1 clove garlic, minced
1 Tbsp. lemon juice
4 cups butternut squash or carrots, shredded
2 cups jicama, shredded
4 cups Napa or Asian cabbage, cut into fine shreds
4 ounces spinach leaves, cut into fine shreds
2 large fresh basil leaves, cut into fine shreds
1/2 cup cilantro (Chinese parsley), cut into fine shreds
2 green onions, finely sliced
1/8 cup chopped peanuts

1. Warm coconut milk to no more than 118 degrees; and add garlic and curry.
2. Toss with remaining ingredients.
3. Form nests in individual shallow bowls or serving dishes and garnish with peanuts and onions.
4. Serve at room temperature or gently warmed in the oven.

Insights: To shred leaves, such as basil and spinach, stack one on top of the other and roll them tightly from stem to tip. Holding them firmly in this rolled position, cut thin slices, starting on one side and working over to the other side, until long, thin strands are completed; then unroll.

Chinese Bean Sprouts Bon Bon

serves 4–6

1 1/2 cups mixed young bean sprouts (see pg. 9)
6 dried shiitake mushrooms, soaked in water for 1 hour
(reserve soaking liquid)
1/4 cup young pumpkin seed sprouts (see pg. 8)
1/4 cup young sunflower seed sprouts (see pg. 8)
1/4 cup walnuts, soaked 12 hours and rinsed
1 sweet red bell pepper, seeded and julienned
1/2 stalk celery, diced
1/2 cup cucumber, diced
1 green onion, thinly sliced
1/3–1/2 cup *Bon Bon Sauce* (see recipe below)
1/4 Napa or Asian cabbage, shredded (optional)

1. Remove shiitake mushrooms from water, squeezing out
   excess. Save liquid for future use in broth or gravy. Cut stems
   from mushrooms and discard. Slice julienne-style.
2. Combine all ingredients together and toss well.
3. If desired, serve on a bed of cabbage.

Bon Bon Sauce

3 Tbsp. raw tahini (sesame seed butter)
1 Tbsp. fresh ginger root, peeled and grated
1 Tbsp. lemon juice
1 Tbsp. maple syrup
1 Tbsp. tamari soy sauce (or, to taste)
1/2 clove garlic, crushed
3 Tbsp. purified water (approx.)

1. Combine ingredients together in hand blender and purée until
   smooth, adding more or less water as needed.

One of my favorite recipes to take to potlucks, this brightly flavored dish always receives applause! It's high in protein and fiber and the *Bon Bon Sauce* is exquisite! You can also use this sauce as a mayonnaise for sandwiches or as a dressing for salads and slaws.

*Guardian Angel,
please help me
focus my desires
so they are in
the best interest
of all concerned.*

Holidays require tradition and in our family that means mushroom roast on Thanksgiving and Christmas! It is heaven for mushroom lovers and is great left over for sandwiches! I generally serve it with *Sesame Tahini Gravy*, but *Onion-Shiitake* and *Mushroom-Almond Gravy* are also recommended. (See pg. 172, 173.)

Guardian Angel,
please help me
allow Divine Love to
permeate my being.

Savory Mushroom Roast with Sesame Tahini Gravy

serves 6–8

12 cups mushrooms, chopped (divided use)
1/2 cup purified water (divided use)
1 large onion, peeled and chopped
olive oil cooking spray
1 1/2 tsp. poultry seasoning
1 1/2 tsp. Vege-Sal® (or 1 tsp. sea salt)
1/2 tsp. celery seed, crushed
3 Tbsp. whole wheat flour
3 Tbsp. gluten flour
6 slices whole wheat bread, diced and toasted
1 Tbsp. unbleached flour

1. Heat a non-stick or stainless steel skillet to medium and add 1/4 cup water. Cook 1/2 of the mushrooms until they are well cooked and dry. Place them in a food processor and purée.
2. Cook the remaining mushrooms in a 1/4 cup of water. Place them in a large bowl and set aside.
3. Spray the pan with oil and sauté the onion until soft and transparent, adding small amounts of water, as needed, to prevent sticking. Put half of the onions in the blender with the puréed mushrooms and the other half in the bowl with the rest of the cooked mushrooms.
4. Put the Vege-Sal®, poultry seasoning and celery seed in the blender with the puréed mushrooms and process the mixture.

5. Preheat oven to 350 degrees.

6. Thoroughly mix the two flours together and add them to the mushrooms and onions in the bowl. Stir well, using your hands if necessary.

7. Add the blended mushroom mixture and the diced bread to the bowl and mix thoroughly.

8. Line the bottom of a loaf pan with foil or parchment paper. Spray with oil and dust with unbleached flour. Pour mixture in and pat smooth.

9. Bake for 1 hour, covered, at 350 degrees. Remove cover and bake another 5 minutes.

10. Remove from oven and allow to rest for 5 minutes before removing from pan. Rest for another 10 minutes before slicing. Serve hot with *Sesame Tahini Gravy* or cold in sandwiches with all the trimmings.

Sesame Tahini Gravy

serves 4

2 Tbsp. tahini (sesame seed butter)
2 Tbsp. tamari soy sauce
2 cups purified water
1/4 cup unbleached flour
1/4 tsp. garlic powder

1. Combine ingredients and blend thoroughly.
2. Simmer to thicken, adding more water if necessary.

Sesame tahini comes raw or toasted. I prefer to use the raw tahini because of the higher enzyme content, but if you are going to cook it, either one will be fine. The flavors are different, so try both kinds and see which one you like.

*Guardian Angel,
I welcome you
into my life
and ask that you
guide and protect me.*

Butternut squash adds a gentle sweetness to the cauliflower in this unusual mashed potato-like dish. I suggest heating it slightly and serving it with warm *Onion-Shiitake Gravy*.

*Guardian Angel,
please help me
invite all energies of
Light and Love into
my life now.*

Squashed Cauliflower with Onion Shiitake Gravy

serves 4

2 cups butternut squash, peeled, seeded, and diced
1 whole cauliflower, cleaned, cored, and chopped
1/4 cup *Almond* or *Cashew Cheese* (see pg. 22, 23)
1 Tbsp. flax oil (optional)
1 Tbsp. Braggs Liquid Aminos® (or sea salt, to taste)
1 Tbsp. white miso paste
dash ground nutmeg and white pepper

1. Place ingredients in a food processor and purée until smooth.
2. Serve like mashed potatoes, at room temperature or slightly warmed, with *Onion Shiitake Gravy.*

Onion Shiitake Gravy

serves 4

4–6 dried shiitake mushrooms
1/4 cup warm purified water
1/4 cup raw tahini (sesame seed butter)
2 Tbsp. Onion Magic® seasoning
1/2 Tbsp. Braggs Liquid Aminos®

1. Soak mushrooms in warm water for 20 minutes. Drain the mushrooms and reserve soaking liquid. Remove stems discard. Mince mushrooms and set aside.
2. Strain sand from mushroom soaking water and combine liquid with remaining ingredients, except for mushrooms. Blend until smooth, add mushrooms, and stir well.
3. Serve at room temperature or slightly warmed, over *Squashed Cauliflower* (see recipe above), mashed potatoes, loaves, or patties.

Cauliflower Pilaf with Mushroom-Almond Gravy

serves 4

1 whole cauliflower, cleaned, cored, and chopped
6 mushrooms, diced
1 small carrot, shredded
1 small stalk celery, diced
1/4 red bell pepper, seeded, and diced
1 small green onion, thinly sliced
1/4 cup *Seasoned Sunflower Seeds* (see pg. 65)
4 tsp. barley miso paste, dissolved in 4 tsp. water
1/2 tsp. poultry seasoning

1. Place cauliflower in food processor and "pulse" grind until it becomes the texture of rice.
2. Remove to a bowl and stir in remaining ingredients.
3. Serve with warm *Mushroom-Almond Gravy*.

Mushroom-Almond Gravy

serves 4–6

olive oil cooking spray or 1/2 tsp. olive oil
1 Tbsp. shallots, minced
2 cups mushrooms, minced
2 Tbsp. each toasted almond butter and barley miso paste
1/4 cup oatmeal flour or unbleached flour
2 cups purified water

1. Heat non-stick skillet and season with oil. Sauté shallots and mushrooms until tender, adding small amounts of water, as needed, to prevent sticking.
2. Combine remaining ingredients in a blender and purée.
3. Simmer purée and mushroom mixture until thick.

I invented this recipe for a grain-sensitive friend who really missed her favorite pilaf. It's quick and easy to make and can be served with or without gravy. We especially like it warmed with this creamy *Mushroom-Almond Gravy*.

Guardian Angel, please assist me in breathing in peace for myself and breathing out peace for the planet.

Naturally sweet and creamy, this fresh corn "Risotto" is delectable as a main course or as a side dish. If you love corn and have only eaten it cooked, you'll be pleasantly surprised at how good it is uncooked!

Guardian Angel,
please help me become
increasingly aware
of your
Light and Love.

Italian-Style
Fresh Corn Risotto

serves 4

4 ears fresh corn, kernels removed from cob (divided use)
1 tsp. light miso
1/2 tsp. nutritional yeast
pinch of white pepper and sea salt
1 Tbsp. *Almond Cheese* (see pg. 22)
3 Tbsp. red onion, diced
2 Tbsp. celery, diced
1/4 cup sweet red pepper, diced
6 fresh mushrooms, diced

1. In blender or food processor, cream 2 cups of corn with cheese, miso, yeast, salt, and pepper.
2. Stir in remaining ingredients and allow to sit for 1 hour.
3. If possible prior to serving, stir again to fluff mixture; serve at room temperature or gently heated in a warm oven.

Insights: Choose commercially grown button mushrooms with the undersides (gills) tightly closed. The skins should be smooth and powdery, not moist and shiny. Trim the ends of the stems, and wipe the caps with a paper towel. If you are preparing a lot of mushrooms for cooking, wash them under water, one at a time holding them upright, so the underside is not exposed; then dry with a towel. Never soak mushrooms in water. If the stems are not needed in the recipe, retain them for later use in making soups, grain dishes, or gravies. Store fresh mushrooms in a paper, cloth, or mesh bag in the refrigerator.

Nebraska Corn Fritters

serves 4

4 ears fresh corn, kernels removed from cob
2 Tbsp. vegan egg replacer (Ener-G brand®)
6 Tbsp. purified water
4 Tbsp. whole wheat pastry flour or unbleached flour
1/2 tsp. sea salt
1/8 tsp. white pepper
1 tsp. peanut oil

1. Combine ingredients, except oil, and stir well.
2. Heat skillet to medium and add oil. Form corn fritters by dropping 2 tablespoons of corn mixture into skillet and pressing down to shape. Allow a little space between each for ease of turning.
3. Cook for 2 to 3 minutes and turn over. Cook another 2 to 3 minutes and remove from pan.
4. Keep warm in oven until serving time. Serve alone or with *Sweet Red Pepper Sauce* (see pg. 162) or *Onion-Shiitake Gravy* (see pg. 172) on the side.

Miles and miles of corn fields create endless ideas for delicious uses for corn. One of my favorites, are corn fritters. They are nurturing and flavorful, and if you have any left over, they're great in sandwiches, too!

*Guardian Angel,
please help me
bask in the radiance
of your Divine Light.*

Potatoes, mushrooms, and vegetables unite in this quick and easy lunch or dinner. You can vary the seasonings to create a whole new taste sensation every time you make it. Try curry powder, chili powder, Italian herbs, or whatever suits your fancy.

Guardian Angel,
please help me
tap into ideas
that are beyond my
knowledge
and experience.

French Oven-Roasted Vegetables

serves 4

4 new potatoes, cleaned and cut into 1-inch chunks
12 large mushrooms, cut into halves
1 medium eggplant, sliced 1 1/2 x 1 1/2-inch chunks
2 zucchini, sliced 1 1/2-inch thick
1 large onion, quartered and separated
2 red bell peppers, seeded and cut into
    1 1/2 x 1 1/2-inch pieces
4 cloves garlic, minced
1 tsp. paprika
1/2 tsp. onion powder
olive oil cooking spray
sea salt to taste
freshly ground black pepper

1. Toss all ingredients together, except oil, salt, and pepper, making sure to coat each vegetable with seasoning.
2. Spray baking sheet with olive oil spray and place vegetables evenly on top. Bake in a preheated 375 degree oven for 30 to 40 minutes.
3. Season to taste with salt and pepper and arrange attractively on each plate. Serve hot or at room temperature.

East Indian Dahl (Curry-Spiced Lentils)

serves 4

olive oil cooking spray or 1/2 tsp. olive oil
1 medium onion, chopped
3 cloves garlic, crushed
1 tsp. ground coriander
1/2 tsp. ground cumin
1/8 tsp. cayenne pepper
1/2 tsp. ground turmeric
1 medium, ripe tomato, peeled and minced
1 tsp. paprika
1/2 tsp. *Garam Masala* (see pg. 150)
1/2 tsp. sea salt (or, to taste)
1 tsp. lemon juice
1 tsp. hot green chili, seeded and minced
1 tsp. fresh ginger root, peeled and grated
2 cups cooked red or yellow lentils
1/4–1/2 cup liquid (water or lentil broth)

1. Heat non-stick skillet to medium-hot and season with oil. Sauté onions and garlic until golden brown, adding small amounts of water, as needed, to prevent sticking.
2. Reduce heat and add coriander, cumin, cayenne, and turmeric. Stir for a few seconds and add tomatoes. Mix well.
3. Add remaining ingredients, using as much water as needed to form a thick consistency, and stir. Cover, and simmer on low heat for 10 to 15 minutes.
4. Serve hot over any cooked rice or grain dish.

East Indians have a way with spices that is unsurpassed. This fragrant, flavorful, traditional lentil dish is a perfect example. *Garam Masala* (see pg. 150) is a seasoning that can be found in specialty markets and, like curry, varies according to the chef.

Guardian Angel, please help me merge with the "All Knowing Mind."

Sprouted, seasoned, and then dehydrated garbanzo beans are used to make these deliciously spicy, unfired falafels. They are served wrapped in cabbage leaves with lettuce or sprouts, chopped tomatoes, and a little *Sesame Dipping Sauce.*

*Guardian Angel,
please help me
bring the energy of
heaven into my
earthly consciousness.*

Live Falafels
(Lebanese-Style Garbanzo Patties)

serves 4 (16 small patties)

2 cups *Middle Eastern Seasoned Garbanzo Nuts*
　(see pg. 64)
2 Tbsp. minced red onion
2 Tbsp. minced fresh parsley
1/4 tsp. each ground cumin and ground coriander
1 clove garlic, crushed
1/2 Tbsp. lemon juice
1/8 tsp. cayenne pepper

1. Purée ingredients together in a food processor until smooth.
2. Divide mixture into 16 portions. Begin by compressing each portion between your palms using your hands clasped together. With your thumb, press around the edge of the patty to form a circle and strengthen it as much as possible.
3. Wrap patties in cabbage or pita bread with a little *Sesame Dipping Sauce*, chopped tomato, and alfalfa sprouts.

Sesame Dipping Sauce

serves 4

6 Tbsp. raw tahini (sesame seed butter)
1–2 cloves of garlic, crushed
1/4 cup lemon juice
1/4 tsp. sea salt
3–4 Tbsp. purified water (approx.)

1. Combine first 4 ingredients and mix well.
2. Slowly blend in enough water to form a thick sauce.
3. Serve at room temperature.

Falafels
(Traditional Garbanzo Patties)

serves 4 (makes 16 small patties)

1 cup dried garbanzo beans, soak in 1 qt. water overnight
1 tsp. baking soda
1 tsp. sea salt
1 medium onion, minced
2 Tbsp. fresh minced parsley or 1 Tbsp. dried parsley
1 tsp. each ground cumin and ground coriander
2 cloves garlic, crushed
1 Tbsp. lemon juice
1/8 tsp. cayenne pepper
olive oil cooking spray or 1 Tbsp. olive oil (divided use)

1. Drain garbanzo beans in colander. Rinse and drain again.
2. Combine garbanzo beans, salt, and soda in a food processor or blender, and process until it is the consistency of coarse flour.
3. Remove garbanzo bean mixture from food processor and combine with other ingredients, except oil. Mix well.
4. Divide mixture into 16 portions. Begin by compressing each portion between your palms, with your hands clasped together. Using your thumb, press around the edge of the patty to form a circle and strengthen it as much as possible. They will barely hold together. Place patties on a platter until all are completed.
5. Heat skillet to medium-hot and add half oil or a spray of oil.
6. Carefully slide 8 patties into the skillet and brown on one side. Turn patties and cover. (The other side will brown as they steam cook.) Set these aside and cook the other 8 patties, as directed above.
7. Serve hot, as an entree, or for a Middle Eastern sandwich, serve in pita bread with *Sesame Dipping Sauce* (see opposite page), chopped tomato, and lettuce.

Traditionally, falafels are deep fried, but this modern low-fat version allows us to enjoy them without guilt. Serve warm in pita bread with chopped lettuce or sprouts, tomatoes, and *Sesame Dipping Sauce*. (See recipe on opposite page.)

Guardian Angel, please help me experience a higher vibration of wisdom and understanding.

Next time you think bar-beque, think tofu steaks. This flavorful *Sesame Miso Glaze* transforms the bland taste of tofu into a delight for the senses! You can also use it on zucchini, eggplant, or summer squash. Simply slice veggies one-inch thick and skip the first step.

Guardian Angel,
please help me
cultivate faith,
courage, and love.

Japanese Broiled Tofu with Sesame-Miso Glaze

serves 4

20 ounces extra-firm tofu, cut into 8 equal-size steaks
1 Tbsp. sea salt

Sesame-Miso Glaze:
1/4 cup mugi miso or hatcho miso
3 Tbsp. tahini (sesame seed butter)
1 Tbsp. Aji Mirin® sweet cooking rice wine
2 tsp. brown rice syrup (or other sweetener)
2 tsp. fresh ginger root, grated
1 clove garlic, crushed
1/2 tsp. toasted sesame oil

1. Place tofu in pan with salt and enough water to cover. Simmer for 20 minutes. When tofu has cooked, carefully remove and drain. Set tofu on paper towels or a clean cloth, and place on an angled surface with a weight on top to press out any remaining liquid. Leave to drain for 15 minutes.
2. Preheat barbeque, grill, or broiler as desired. Oil grill, if necessary.
3. Combine ingredients for *Sesame-Miso Glaze* and cream thoroughly.
4. Barbeque, grill, or broil tofu until it begins to brown. Turn over and paint the top with *Sesame-Miso Glaze,* 1/8-inch thick. (Add a few drops of water if the paste is too thick.) Turn again and paint a thin layer of glaze on the opposite side. If heat source is from below, turn once more to cook both sides of tofu. Serve hot.

Hawaiian Teriyaki Tempeh Brochettes

serves 4

Teriyaki Sauce:
1/3 cup lime juice or rice vinegar
1/3 cup soy sauce
1 tsp. sesame oil
1 1/2 Tbsp. Aji Mirin® sweet cooking rice wine
2 Tbsp. pure maple syrup or molasses
1 small clove garlic, crushed
1/2 tsp. fresh ginger root, crushed or finely grated
1 Tbsp. arrowroot, dissolved in 1/4 cup water

20–24 ounces tempeh, cut into 1-inch cubes
2 bell peppers, seeded and cut into bite-size chunks
20-ounce can sliced pineapple, cut into large chunks
1 large red onion, cut into eighths and
    separated into layers
12–16 mushrooms

Bamboo skewers, soaked in water for 1/2 hour

1. Combine ingredients for sauce, except arrowroot and water.
2. Simmer tempeh in sauce for 15 minutes, turning over once.
3. Remove tempeh and place on bamboo skewers, alternating with onions, mushrooms, peppers, and pineapple.
4. Place under hot broiler or on charcoal grill until vegetables are cooked, about 15 minutes.
5. While brochettes are cooking, bring remaining sauce to a simmer and add arrowroot-water mixture. Cook for a minute or two until just thickened, and remove.
6. A few minutes before brochettes have finished cooking, generously brush thickened sauce over all sides of tempeh and vegetables. Serve hot.

These brochettes are great for barbeques, as they are both beautiful and delicious. Tofu can be substituted for tempeh, and you may use any seasonal vegetables that will hold their shape when skewered.

Guardian Angel, please help me appreciate life and all its blessings.

Thai Stir-Fried Rice Noodles

serves 4

Delicate rice noodles have a unique texture and flavor and are perfect for noodle lovers! Combined with the pungent flavor of garlic, chilies, and shiitake mushrooms, this typical Thai specialty is out of this world!

*Guardian Angel,
please help me
recognize that
each moment is
a sacred experience.*

8 ounces flat rice sticks, cooked according to directions
olive oil cooking spray or 1/2 tsp. toasted sesame oil
1 onion, julienned
3 cloves garlic, minced
1–2 carrots, julienned
1/2 large cucumber, peeled, sliced lengthwise, and seeded
1 dried red chili, soaked for 15 to 20 minutes and sliced
4–6 ounces seitan or baked tofu, julienned
1 pound fresh bean sprouts
6 dried shiitake mushrooms, soaked 20 minutes and sliced
3 green onions, sliced

Thai Stir-Fry Sauce:
1 Tbsp. tamari soy sauce (or, to taste)
1/2 tsp. toasted sesame oil
1/2 tsp. freshly ground black pepper
3/4 cup reserved shiitake-soaking liquid
1/2 Tbsp. arrowroot
1/4 tsp. fresh ground chili paste (Sambal Oelek®)

1/4 cup peanuts, ground
4 Tbsp. cilantro (Chinese parsley), chopped

1. Heat wok or large skillet to medium-hot and season with oil. Add onions and stir-fry for a few minutes, adding small amounts of water, as needed, to prevent sticking. Add garlic and cook another minute.
2. Add carrots and cucumbers and cook 2 to 3 more minutes. Stir in remaining ingredients except sauce and garnishes.
3. Combine ingredients for sauce and add to wok, stirring until mixture begins to thicken.
4. Add hot, cooked noodles to wok and gently toss.
5. Garnish each serving with peanuts and cilantro.

Vietnamese Vegetables & Tofu on Noodles

serves 4

12 ounces ramen noodles
8 dried shiitake mushrooms, soak in water for 20 minutes
2 wood ear mushrooms, soak in water for 20 minutes
olive oil cooking spray or 1/2 tsp. toasted sesame oil
2 cups broccoli, cut into small bite-size pieces
2 carrots, sliced
1/2 green pepper, julienned
1 stalk celery or bok choy, sliced
1/2 medium-size zucchini, julienned
1/4 cabbage, shredded
1 can baby corn, drained and rinsed
1/2 block fried tofu, cut into 1-inch cubes

Garnishes:
1/2 cup finely shredded carrot
1/4 cup peanuts, ground
1/4 tsp. ground chili paste (Sambal Olek®)

1. Read package instructions to determine cooking time for noodles. Noodles must be ready, without being overcooked, when the vegetables are ready to be eaten.
2. Heat wok or non-stick skillet to medium-hot and season with oil. Stir-fry broccoli and carrots for 2 minutes, adding small amounts of water, as needed, to prevent sticking.
3. Remove stems from shiitake mushrooms and discard. Slice shiitake and wood ear mushrooms and add them to the wok along with the remaining vegetables and tofu. Stir-fry for a few more minutes until vegetables are cooked, yet still crisp.
4. Serve vegetables over individual bowls of hot noodles and garnish each with carrot, peanuts, and a pinch of chili paste.

Often, people confuse Thai and Vietnamese foods, and it's no wonder; compare these two dishes and you'll see definite similarities. Bu'n Chay, as this is called in Vietnam is made with wheat "ramen" noodles and served with the veggies on top. It makes a great lunch or dinner.

Guardian Angel,
please help me
let go of doubt and
share messages of hope.

The combination of noodles and sesame is difficult to resist. This delightfully simple recipe is a delicious and satisfying summer lunch or dinner.

Guardian Angel, please help me encourage and inspire others.

Japanese Buckwheat Noodles with Sesame

serves 4

8 ounces buckwheat-yam soba noodles,
    cooked according to package directions
2 Tbsp. tamari soy sauce (or, to taste)
1/2 cup *Shiitake Dashi* (see pg. 133)
2 Tbsp. maple syrup or Sucanat®
    (dehydrated sugar cane juice)
2 Tbsp. tahini (sesame seed butter)
1 pound fresh asparagus or green beans, cut at an angle
    into 1-inch lengths
4 green onions, cut at an angle into 1-inch lengths
toasted sesame seeds

1. Combine soy sauce, dashi, syrup, and tahini, and purée.
2. Rinse cooked soba noodles in ice water and drain thoroughly. Toss soy sauce mixture with noodles and chill.
3. Blanch asparagus or green beans in boiling water until just cooked, about 4 minutes. Rinse in ice water and drain thoroughly.
4. Toss vegetables and green onions with noodles and place in refrigerator until well chilled. Garnish with sesame seeds prior to serving.

Angel Hair Pasta with Asparagus and Morels

serves 4

1 pound angel hair pasta

olive oil cooking spray or 1/2 tsp. olive oil
2/3 pound fresh morels, cleaned and quartered lengthwise
2 Tbsp. shallots, minced
1 large leek, washed thoroughly and thinly sliced
2 cups fresh asparagus, sliced diagonally
   into 2-inch lengths
2 large red bell peppers, roasted, peeled,
   seeded, and julienned
1/2 cup dry white wine
2 Tbsp. dijon-style prepared mustard
sea salt and pepper to taste
1/4 cup toasted pine nuts or slivered almonds

1. Heat non-stick skillet to medium and season with oil. Add morels, shallots, leeks, and asparagus. Sauté until soft, about 6 to 8 minutes, adding small amounts of water, as needed, to prevent sticking.
2. Meanwhile, boil water for pasta and cook according to package directions.
3. Add remaining ingredients to skillet and simmer for 5 minutes. Adjust salt and pepper to taste.
4. Toss mixture with hot cooked pasta and garnish with nuts. Serve immediately.

Asparagus and morels make this pasta dish a special spring delight. It's light and easy to prepare this masterpiece of simplicity!

Guardian Angel, please help me learn and evolve through my daily lessons.

A meal in itself, this favorite of the "Enlightened One" could become a favorite of yours, too! Vary the vegetables according to your taste and substitute tofu or tempeh to create your own version.

*Guardian Angel,
please help me
recognize challenges
as valuable
learning experiences.*

*Buddha's Garden
(Chinese Vegetables with Seitan)*
serves 4

8 ounces chuka soba (oriental-style noodles), cooked according to manufacturer's directions
4 large dried shiitake mushrooms and 3 dried tree ear fungus, soaked in 2 cups hot water (reserve liquid)

Buddha's Sauce:
1/2 tsp. sesame oil
2 tsp. minced peeled ginger
1/4 cup tamari soy sauce
1/4 cup Aji Mirin® rice wine
1/4 tsp. ground chili paste (Sombal Olek®)
1 cup reserved mushroom-soaking liquid
3 Tbsp. arrowroot or cornstarch plus 3 Tbsp. cold water

olive oil cooking spray or 1/2 tsp. toasted sesame oil
2 tsp. peeled ginger root, very thinly sliced and julienned
2 medium carrots, julienned
1/2 bell pepper, julienned
2 small zucchinis, julienned
4 ounces water chestnuts or 1/2 cup jicama, julienned
2 cups wheat gluten (seitan), rinsed, drained and julienned
2 cups fresh bean sprouts or 1 1/2 cups shredded cabbage
6 scallions, shredded lengthwise then cut on the diagonal, about 2-inches long

1. Cook soba noodles, drain, and rinse well with cold water, then drain again and set aside.
2. Squeeze excess moisture from mushrooms and reserve the soaking liquid. Remove and discard stems, and slice.
3. Combine ingredients for sauce and set aside.
4. Heat a non-stick skillet or wok to medium and season with oil. Gently cook 2 tsp. minced ginger. Remove from pan, and combine with the remaining sauce ingredients in a small bowl. Set aside.
5. Add vegetables to wok and begin stir-frying vegetables and previously soaked mushrooms in order of length of time required to cook. Allow carrots to cook for 1 minute before adding peppers and zucchini. After another minute add other ingredients and heat well.
6. Rinse and drain noodles again. Carefully stir in noodles and sauce, stirring continuously until sauce is thick and mixture is hot throughout. Serve immediately.

Insights: Seitan, sometimes called wheat meat, is a high protein product made from wheat gluten flour. It can be made at home, with a little effort, or purchased from a health food or specialty store. The texture is very meaty and it can be used in many recipes calling for meat. Because of it's web-like nature and delicate flavor, it becomes a sponge for a variety of seasonings.

In this recipe, I prefer to use the long, Oriental bean sprouts which are available in Asian markets and many grocery stores.

Guardian Angel, thank you for sharing with me your Light, Love and Devotion.

Chapter Ten

Divine Desserts

A Talk with Spirit about Love

Dear One, please help me love and be loved unconditionally. Assist me in knowing that I am worthy and deserving of love. I desire to let go of the fear of rejection, which keeps love away. Help me to open my heart and allow the healing power of love to flow in. My intention is to see the Divine in everyone and everything so I may freely love them. Please assist me in looking for the spark of God in each person I meet. Help me see my own Light and allow it to shine freely, so I may become a beacon for others.

I feel the presence of love in this food and am thankful for the nourishment I receive from it. I allow this love and gratitude to expand within my heart, filling me with Divine Light. I love you, I bless you, I am one with you and All That Is.

Recipes at a Glance

Divine Desserts

If you love cookies, but you don't like to bake, these unfired cookie recipes are for you! The longer they stay in the dehydrator, the more crunchy they become. They make great pie crusts, too!

Guardian Angel, please assist me in my communions with nature and the Divine.

Sweet Nut'ins

makes 4 dozen cookies or 2 soft pie crusts

2 cups whole raw almonds, soaked for 24 hours, rinsed and drained
1 cup walnuts, soaked for 12 hours, rinsed and drained
3 cups pitted dates, coarsely chopped
3/4 tsp. orange or almond extract

1. Place all ingredients in a food processor. Using the "S" blade, grind until mixture begins to stick together.
2. Taking a tablespoon of the mixture for each, roll into little balls using the palm of your hand.
3. Flatten the balls and lay them out on a drying sheet in the dehydrator and allow to dry for 24 hours. Or, place them on a cookie sheet in the oven on a warm setting for 8 to 12 hours or until the cookies are as firm and crisp as desired.
4. Store cookies in an airtight container in the refrigerator or in a cool place. They will keep for up to three months.

Macadamia Banana Coconut Cookies

makes 4 dozen cookies or 2 pie crusts

2 cups raw macadamia nuts, soaked for 24 hours, rinsed
   and drained
1 cup almonds, soaked for 24 hours, rinsed and drained
1 cup pitted dates, coarsely chopped
1/4 tsp. almond extract
2 ripe bananas
1/2 cup natural, unsweetened, dried coconut

1. Place nuts, dates, and almond extract in a food processor.
   Using the "S" blade, grind until mixture begins to stick together. Add bananas and process to form a dough. Stir in
   coconut.
2. Drop by the tablespoon onto a drying sheet and dehydrate
   for 24 hours. Or, place cookies on a cookie sheet in the oven
   at the lowest setting for 8 to 12 hours or until the cookies
   are as firm and crisp as desired.
3. Store cookies in an airtight container in the refrigerator or in
   a cool place. Refrigerated, they will keep for up to three
   months.

No need to worry about burning these cookies, since they aren't actually cooked! The amount of time in the dehydrator determines the texture. Soft and moist, they are delectable. Firm and crisp, they are incredible!

*Guardian Angel,
please help me
align myself with the
frequencies of Light.*

The combination of apricots and almonds in this chewy cookie is delightful. In fact, if you can't wait, this is a great cookie to eat raw!

Guardian Angel,
please help me be
a perfect example of
what humanity can be.

Apricot Almond Cookies

makes 4 dozen cookies or 2 soft pie crusts

2 cups whole raw almonds, soaked for 24 hours, rinsed
   and drained
1 cup walnuts, soaked for 12 hours, rinsed and drained
1 cup pitted dates, coarsely chopped
2 cups unsulfured, dried apricots, chopped

1. Place all ingredients in a food processor. Using the "S" blade, grind until mixture begins to stick together.
2. Taking a tablespoon of the mixture for each, roll into little balls using the palm of your hand.
3. Flatten the balls and lay them out on a drying sheet in the dehydrator and allow to dry for 24 hours. Or, place them on a cookie sheet in the oven on a warm setting for 8 to 12 hours or until the cookies are as firm and crisp as desired.
4. Store cookies in an airtight container in the refrigerator or in a cool place. Refrigerated, they will keep for up to three months.

Carob Date Cookies

makes 4 dozen cookies or 2 soft pie crusts

2 cups whole raw almonds, soaked for 24 hours, rinsed
    and drained
1 cup walnuts, soaked for 12 hours, rinsed and drained
3 cups pitted dates, coarsely chopped
1/2 cup untoasted, unsweetened, carob powder
2 Tbsp. powdered grain beverage (coffee substitute)
1/4 tsp. ground cinnamon

1. Place all ingredients in a food processor. Using the "S" blade,
   grind until mixture sticks together, adding small amounts
   of water, if needed, to hold it together.
2. Taking a tablespoon of the mixture for each, roll into little
   balls using the palm of your hand. (If the mixture is too wet,
   simply drop by the tablespoon, as you would cookie dough.)
3. Flatten the balls and lay them out on a drying sheet in the
   dehydrator and allow to dry for 24 hours. Or, place the cookies on a cookie sheet in the oven on the lowest setting for 8
   to 12 hours or until the cookies are as crisp as desired.
4. Store cookies in an airtight container in the refrigerator or in
   a cool place. Refrigerated, they will keep for up to three
   months.

Carob, or St. John's Bread, has been around for centuries. (It is even mentioned in the Bible.) It may taste devilish, but it's really heavenly!

*Guardian Angel,
please help me
recognize my inner
beauty and radiate it
outwardly.*

Gooey and chewy or firm and crisp—it all depends on how long these cookies remain in the dehydrator/oven. Kids love them!

Guardian Angel,
please help me see
the expression of
Light in everyone
and everything.

Sesame Cashew Chews

makes 4 dozen chewy cookies

1/2 cup molasses
1/2 cup brown rice syrup
2 Tbsp. apple cider vinegar
1 Tbsp. peanut or corn oil
1/2 tsp. sea salt
2 cups whole raw sesame seeds
1 cup cashew pieces

1. Heat liquid ingredients and add salt. Simmer gently, stirring often, until mixture become very thick, about 5 to 7 minutes. Allow to cool slightly.
2. Add seeds and cashews to the liquid and stir. Mixture should be thick and sticky.
3. Drop by the tablespoon onto a drying sheet and dehydrate for 24 hours. Or, place the cookies on a cookie sheet in the oven on the lowest setting for 8 to 12 hours or until the cookies are as crisp as desired.
4. Store cookies in an airtight container in the refrigerator or in a cool place. Refrigerated, they will keep for up to three months.

Almond Fig Biscuits with Apricot Coulis

serves 4

2 cups whole raw almonds, soaked for 8 to 12 hours,
  rinsed and drained
1 cup walnuts, soaked for 8 to 12 hours, rinsed and
  drained
3 cups dried figs, soaked in warm water for 1 hour,
  drained, and chopped
16 fresh ripe apricots, pitted (room temperature)
1/2 cup fresh apple juice (room temperature)
1/8 tsp. cinnamon
dash of nutmeg
4 sprigs fresh mint

1. Place first 3 ingredients in a food processor. Using the "S" blade, grind until mixture holds together.
2. Taking 2 tablespoons of the mixture for each, roll into balls in the palm of your hand.
3. Flatten the balls to form small biscuits and place in oven on low for 1 to 2 hours.
4. Just before serving, purée remaining ingredients, except mint, and pour evenly onto 4 individual dessert dishes. Place 2 biscuits on top of each. Garnish with a sprig of mint and serve. Store extra biscuits in an airtight container in the refrigerator, or if preferred, dehydrate to form firm cookies.

If you want to make a special treat but can't start a day ahead, these biscuits are easy and quick to prepare, yet look and taste really special.

*Guardian Angel,
please help me
experience life
joyfully .*

If you like carob, this will satisfy your sweet tooth! The coffee substitute and cinnamon give this candy a chocolaty flavor without the chocolate. It's hard to believe that something so delicious can be so good for you!

Guardian Angel,
please help me know
that Universal Law
expresses itself
in my life.

Carob Nut Candy

makes 16 squares

1 1/2 cups raw Brazil nuts, soaked 24 hours, rinsed, drained, and ground
1 1/2 cups raw almonds, soaked 24 hours, rinsed, drained, and ground
1/2 cup brown rice syrup
1/3 cup Sucanat® (dehydrated sugar cane juice)
1 cup untoasted, unsweetened carob powder
1/2 cup powdered instant grain beverage (coffee substitute)
1 1/2 tsp. ground cinnamon
1 tsp. vanilla extract

1. Combine ingredients in a food processor and purée until smooth.
2. Press firmly into an 8-inch square baking dish and chill for at least 2 hours.
3. Cut into 2-inch squares and serve chilled or frozen.

Moroccan Almond-Stuffed Dates

makes 3 dozen

3 Tbsp. brown rice syrup
1/4 tsp. orange extract or 1 Tbsp. orange blossom
   water
1 cup raw almonds, ground to a fine powder
36 whole pitted dates, slit lengthwise on one side

1. Mix rice syrup and orange extract together. Add to almond meal.
2. Stuff each date with 1/2 tsp. of the mixture and serve. Will keep in refrigerator a week or more in an airtight container.

Insights: Dates come in a variety of sizes, colors and flavors. Some are very dry, while others are wet and sticky. For stuffing, I suggest Madjool dates, because of their size and texture. When removing the pit from the date, visually inspect the inside to be certain it does not contain insect droppings. If it does, discard it. Fortunately, one bad date does not spoil the batch!

Dates were considered to be one of the seven holy fruits of the Essenes. It's easy to see why. They are so sweet and luscious! This recipe is a traditional one, very similar to the way the Essenes would have prepared it.

*Guardian Angel,
please help me feel the
omnipresence of God
"The One"
within my own body.*

Many different cultures throughout the world use naturally sweet root vegetables as a base for candies. You'll understand why when you taste this wonderful, sweet candy with a prize cleverly hidden in the center!

*Guardian Angel,
please help me let go of
all feelings that are
contrary to Love.*

Japanese
Sweet Potato Confectionary

makes 2 dozen

12 ounces sweet potatoes, cooked, peeled, and mashed
1 cup Sucanat® (dehydrated sugar cane juice)
1 1/4 cup sweet rice flour
12 canned sweet chestnuts, cut into halves (or use 24 walnut halves)

1. Bring 2 quarts of water to a boil.
2. Meanwhile, combine the mashed sweet potato with the Sucanat® and mix well.
3. Add the rice flour and knead until smooth.
4. Divide the dough into 24 balls of equal size.
5. Press a chestnut half into the center of each ball and pinch the hole closed so that the ball is smooth.
6. When the water has reached a rolling boil, poach the sweet potato balls for 6 minutes. Remove and drain.
7. Chill and enjoy.

Japanese Sweet Azuki Beans

makes 2 cups

2/3 cup azuki beans, washed carefully
1 cup Sucanat® (dehydrated sugar cane juice)

1. Soak beans overnight in 3 cups of water. Drain and add 4 cups more water.
2. Bring to a boil, cover, and turn off heat. Allow to rest for 1 hour.
3. Add Sucanat® and simmer, covered, for 30 minutes, or until beans are tender. Remove lid and cook another 15 minutes. Allow to cool in broth, then, drain and chill.

Insights: Sucanat® is a whole food sweetener with a brown sugar taste. After the cane is juiced, it is flash-dried to retain flavor, vitamins, and minerals. Use it to sweeten anything calling for sugar. But remember, its distinctive flavor can overtake more delicate flavors, and it can color a dish with its warm brown hues.

I first tasted sweet azuki beans in Hawaii and was surprised how good they were. This Japanese-inspired treat is as simple as can be and is a great high-protein snack for the kids when they get home from school!

Guardian Angel, please help me be in the moment, every moment.

Yum! Summer doesn't get much better than this! This fresh fruit pie is so healthful, why not just make an evening meal out of it?!

Guardian Angel, please help me become a beacon of Light to others.

Fresh Peach & Berry Pie

serves 8

Crust:
 1/2 recipe of *Sweet Nut'ins* (see pg. 190)

Filling:
 5–6 sweet ripe peaches, washed, pitted, and sliced
 1 pint sweet berries of choice, washed and trimmed

Glaze:
 1/3 cup water
 1/2 tsp. agar powder or 1/2 Tbsp. agar flakes
 3 Tbsp. peach or apricot fruit spread

 1 cup sweetened *Almond* or *Cashew Cream* (see
   pg. 16, 17)

1. To prepare the *Sweet Nut'ins Crust*, place ingredients in a food processor. Using the "S" blade, grind until mixture holds together.
2. Press the crust evenly into an 8 to 9 inch torte pan, extending the crust up the sides. (If a firm crust is desired, place in dehydrator, or a warm oven at no more than 118 degrees for 4 to 6 hours.)
3. Layer the peach slices evenly and attractively on top of the crust, bringing them slightly up the sides. Place the berries in the center and distribute out toward the edge, allowing a 2-inch border of peaches.
4. Combine the agar and water in a small saucepan and bring to a boil. Cool slightly and mix in the fruit spread. When the mixture is no warmer than 118 degrees (warm to the touch), pour it evenly over the top of the pie.
5. For an extra-rich treat, serve it with sweetened *Almond* or *Cashew Cream*.

Tropical Fruit Torte

serves 8

Crust:

1/2 recipe of *Macadamia Banana Coconut Cookies* (see pg. 191)

Filling:

6–8 ounces dehydrated pineapple, chopped, and soaked in 2 cups fresh orange juice for 2 hours

2 1/2 bananas, peeled and thinly sliced

2–3 papaya, peeled, seeded and thinly sliced

Glaze:

1/3 cup water

1/2 tsp. agar powder or 1/2 Tbsp. agar flakes

3 Tbsp. pineapple fruit spread

1. To prepare the crust, place ingredients, except bananas, in a food processor. Using the "S" blade, grind until mixture starts to hold together. Add 1/2 banana and process again.
2. Press the crust evenly into a lightly oiled 8 or 9-inch torte pan (or pie pan), extending the crust up the sides. (If a firm crust is desired, place in dehydrator, or a warm oven at no more than 118 degrees for 4 to 6 hours.)
3. Drain the pineapple and place it in a food processor, using the "S" blade, and grind it until it starts to clump together. Place it evenly on top of the crust, pressing gently and allowing a 1-inch border of crust to remain exposed.
4. Layer the banana and papaya slices evenly and attractively on top of the pineapple.
5. Combine the agar and water in a small saucepan and bring to a boil. Cool slightly and mix in the fruit spread. When the mixture is no warmer than 118 degrees (warm to the touch) pour it evenly over the top of the pie and chill.

When you taste this, you'll think you've gone to heaven and it's in Hawaii! The macadamia crust is a perfect compliment to these tropical fruits.

Guardian Angel, please help me accept myself and show others who I really am.

If you love receiving accolades for your gourmet creations, this gourmet delight is well worth the forethought it requires. It is beyond description!

Guardian Angel,
please help me
recognize the joy in
this present moment.

Pear Almond Torte

serves 8

1 recipe *Easy All-Nut Crust* (see pg. 203)

Cheese Filling:
1/2 cup firm, unseasoned *Almond Cheese* (see pg. 22)
3 Tbsp. brown rice syrup
1/2 tsp. almond extract

Glaze:
1/3 cup water
1/2 tsp. agar powder or 1/2 Tbsp. agar flakes
3 Tbsp. apricot fruit spread

3 fresh pears, peeled, cored, and sliced

1. To prepare the crust see following recipe.
2. Press the crust evenly into an 8 or 9-inch torte pan (or pie pan), extending the crust up the sides. (If a firm crust is desired, place in dehydrator, or a warm oven at no more than 118 degrees for 4 to 6 hours.)
3. Spread the *Cheese Filling* on top of the crust and layer the pear slices on top.
4. Combine the agar and water in a small saucepan and bring to a boil. Cool slightly and mix in the fruit spread. When the mixture is no warmer than 118 degrees (warm to the touch), pour it over the top of the pears.
5. Chill for at least 1 hour prior to serving.

Easy All-Nut Crust

makes 1 pie shell

1/2 cup raw almonds
1/2 cup raw pecans or walnuts
corn oil cooking spray

1. Preheat oven to 350 degrees (for prebaked pie shell only).
2. Combine nuts and grind, using a food processor or nut grinder until the mixture begins to stick together.
3. Spray the bottom and sides of an 8-inch pie pan with oil.
4. Press the nut mixture firmly and evenly on the bottom and sides of the pie pan. Spray the top of the crust lightly with oil.
5. If recipe calls for a pre-baked pie shell, bake for 5 to 8 minutes.

Insights: Agar-agar is a processed sea vegetable product which, when dissolved in water, will form a gel much like gelatin. Since gelatin is obtained by boiling animal tissues, agar-agar is the vegetarian choice for aspics, jello-like dishes, and to thicken custards and toppings. It comes in stick form, which needs to be broken apart, soaked, and simmered; flake, which requires soaking and simmering; and powder, which requires only soaking. It is almost tasteless, so it lends itself well to dessert making.

If you shy away from making pies because preparing the crust is messy, time consuming, and full of butter or hydrogenated fat, this recipe is for you! It's easy and delicious!

Guardian Angel,
please help me remain
grounded and peaceful
at all times.

While growing up, I always wondered why adults liked that awful minced meat pie at Thanksgiving. I think this is a version everyone can be thankful for. It's fantastic!

Guardian Angel, please help me feel my connection with the "Infinite Source of All."

Minced Fruit Pie

serves 12

1 precooked 8-inch *Easy All-Nut Crust* (see pg. 203)

Filling:
4 ounces dried apples
4 ounces dried pears
4 ounces dried peaches
4 ounces dried figs
1 1/2 cups orange juice
1/2 cup Grand Marnier® (optional)
2 Tbsp. lemon juice
1/2 tsp. cinnamon
1/2 tsp. allspice
1/2 tsp. nutmeg

1. Remove stems from figs and cores from pears and discard.
2. Combine fruits, liquids, and spices and simmer gently for 40 minutes. Drain fruits, reserving liquid.
3. Preheat oven to 375 degrees.
4. Grind mixture in a food processor, adding small amounts of reserved liquid, if needed, to form a sticky filling. (Mixture should be minced, not puréed.) Spread evenly in pre-baked pie shell.
5. Bake in a preheated oven for 30 minutes. Allow to cool before cutting.

Sweet Potato Pie

serves 8

1 unbaked 8-inch *Easy All-Nut Crust* using almonds and
  pecans (see pg. 203)

Filling:
2 cups yams or sweet potatoes, cooked, peeled and
  mashed
2 Tbsp. unbleached flour
1 tsp. cinnamon
1/2 cup Sucanat® (dehydrated sugar cane juice)

1 cup sweetened *Almond Cream* (see pg. 16)

1. Preheat oven to 350 degrees.
2. Combine all filling ingredients together in a blender or food
   processor and purée until smooth and creamy.
3. Pour sweet potato filling into an unbaked pie shell. Bake for
   30 minutes.
4. Allow to cool thoroughly prior to cutting.
5. If desired, serve with sweetened *Almond Cream*.

When you taste this you'll know why they call it "soul food"! You can be sure this pie won't languish in the refrigerator!

*Guardian Angel,
please help me
remember to
communicate with
the Energies of Light.*

This pie receives applause every time I prepare it. Fresh pumpkin pie is so rich and creamy, you'll never want to use canned pumpkin again.

*Guardian Angel,
please help me
always trust my
intuition.*

Tofu Pumpkin Pie with Cashew Cream Glaze

serves 8

1 unbaked 8-inch *Easy All-Nut Crust* (see pg. 203)

Filling:
2 Tbsp. agar-agar flakes, soaked in 1/4 cup water for 10 minutes
4 cups pumpkin or butternut squash, peeled, seeded, chopped, and steamed
8 ounces firm silken tofu, drained and patted dry
1/2 cup Sucanat® (dehydrated sugar cane juice)
1/2 cup brown rice syrup or maple syrup
1 Tbsp. corn oil
3 Tbsp. arrowroot
1 tsp. ground cinnamon
1/2 tsp. ground nutmeg
1/2 tsp. ground ginger
1/4 tsp. ground cloves
1 tsp. vanilla
1/4 tsp. sea salt

Cashew Cream Glaze (see opposite page)

1. To prepare filling, simmer agar-water for 15 minutes, stirring until dissolved.
2. Preheat oven to 350 degrees.
3. Purée remaining filling ingredients in a blender. Add agar and mix thoroughly.
4. Pour filling mixture into unbaked pie shell and bake in preheated oven for 40 minutes. Cover pie shell with foil, reduce oven heat to 250 degrees, and cook for another 20 minutes. Allow to cool.
5. When pie is cool, prepare glaze. (See following recipe.)

Cashew Cream Glaze

1 Tbsp. agar-agar flakes (or 1 tsp. powdered) soaked in
   1/4 cup water for 10 minutes
2/3 cup raw unsalted cashews
1/3 cup water
1/2 tsp. vanilla
1/3 cup brown rice syrup

1. Simmer agar-water for 15 minutes until agar is thoroughly dissolved.
2. Combine remaining ingredients in a blender and process until smooth and creamy. Add dissolved agar and mix again.
3. Pour glaze evenly over the top of the pie and chill.

Smooth and luscious, this glaze will make you forget how much you used to like whipped cream!

Guardian Angel, please help me remember that I am one with "The One."

This moist, scrumptious, unfired carrot cake even has a "cream cheese" frosting! Everyone I serve it to wants the recipe. It's certain to be a family favorite!

Guardian Angel, please help me anchor Light and be in harmony with Spirit.

Carrot Apple Kuchen
serves 8

Kuchen:
1 cup ground dried apples
30 pitted dates (about 1 cup packed), minced
4 medium carrots, scraped and shredded
4 medium apples, cored and shredded
1/2 cup shredded unsweetened coconut (divided use)
2 tsp. ground cinnamon
1/4 tsp. ground nutmeg

Cream Cheese Frosting:
1/2 cup firm *Almond* or *Cashew Cream Cheese* (see pg. 22, 23)
3 Tbsp. brown rice syrup
1/2 tsp. almond extract

1. Hand mix ingredients for *Kuchen*, reserving 2 tablespoons of coconut, then grind ingredients in food processor.
2. Firmly press *Kuchen* mixture into an 8-inch springform pan or any comparably sized pan.
3. Combine ingredients for frosting and mix well. Spread *Cream Cheese Frosting* evenly on top of cake and top with reserved coconut. Chill for at least 2 hours. Remove from springform pan and serve. Will keep in refrigerator for up to three days.

Apple Spice Kuchen

serves 8

2 cups ground dried apples
4 medium apples, cored and shredded
1 cup young sprouted wheat berries (see pg. 9)
1/2 cup date paste or finely ground dates
1/2 cup almonds
2 tsp. ground cinnamon
1/2 tsp. allspice
1/4 tsp. ground nutmeg
1/4 tsp. ground ginger
1/2 cup dehydrated currents (or chopped raisins)
1/2 cup walnuts
1 cup thick sweetened *Cashew Cream* (see pg. 17—
   optional)

1. Grind ingredients, except currents and walnuts, in food
   processor. Add currents and walnuts, and pulse to mix.
2. Firmly press cake mixture into an 8-inch springform pan
   (or any comparably sized pan).
3. Chill for at least 2 hours. Remove from springform and
   serve. If desired, spoon 2 tablespoons sweetened *Cashew
   Cream* over each slice. Will keep in refrigerator for up to
   three days.

This down-home apple cake tastes a lot like French apple pie. It's great as an after-school treat, or dressed up with sweetened *Cashew Cream* (see page 17) and served in thin slices as an elegant dessert!

*Guardian Angel,
please help me
remember to breathe in
the breath of God.*

This was always my favorite cake when I was a child. I have replaced my mothers butter and eggs with ingredients that suit my present lifestyle. When I make it, the child in me emerges. Yummy!

*Guardian Angel,
please help me
let go of the illusion
of separation and
recognize my Oneness
with all things.*

Hawaiian Pineapple Upside Down Cake

serves 8

Topping:
1 Tbsp. corn oil
1/2 cup Sucanat® (dehydrated sugar cane juice)
2 Tbsp. brown rice syrup
4 slices canned pineapple, drained, reserving liquid
3 Tbsp. pineapple juice (reserved from canned pineapple)

Cake:
2 1/8 cups whole wheat pastry flour
3/4 tsp. baking soda
1/2 tsp. sea salt
1/4 cup corn oil
2 tsp. vegan egg replacer (Ener-G® brand)
1/2 cup granulated fructose or FruitSource®
1/3 cup plain soy milk
1/2 Tbsp. vanilla extract
4 slices canned pineapple, drained and chopped
2/3 cup pineapple juice (reserved from canned pineapple)

1. Coat the bottom of an 8 x 8-inch square glass baking dish, or any comparably sized pan, with 1 tablespoon oil.

2. Sprinkle the Sucanat® evenly over the oil. Drizzle the rice syrup, then 3 tablespoons pineapple juice evenly over the top. Place four pineapple slices on top, press firmly, and set aside.
3. Preheat oven to 375 degrees.
4. Sift together pastry flour, soda, and salt, and set aside.
5. Cream remaining ingredients together, except for the chopped pineapple.
6. Mix liquid and dry ingredients together, and fold in the chopped pineapple.
7. Carefully spread batter evenly over topping.
8. Bake in preheated oven for 30 minutes.
9. Allow cake to rest for 5 minutes. Carefully turn it onto a larger platter. Cool another 1/2 hour prior to cutting. Serve warm or cold.

Insights: Egg replacers often contain egg white, so if you are avoiding animal products, read the package carefully before buying. I use Ener-G®[1] brand egg replacer, which can be purchased at most health foods stores. It's a great thickener, leavener, and binder to use in baking, as well as in cooked sauces.

Usually I shy away from canned foods, but in this case I use canned pineapple because it will be cooked and is guaranteed to be sweet.

Guardian Angel, please help me feel my connectedness with "The One" at all times.

Bananas and coconut just seem to be made for each other! This is a heavenly custard and a great treat to offer all the earthly angels in your house!

*Guardian Angel,
please assist me in
knowing that
I deserve to experience
love, joy, and
harmony in my life.*

Caribbean Banana Coconut Custard

serves 8

1 1/4 cup low-fat plain soy milk
1/4 cup purified water
1/3 cup vegan egg replacer (Ener-G® brand)
1/3 cup Sucanat® (dehydrated sugar cane juice)
1/2 Tbsp. agar-agar powder or 2 tsp. fruit pectin
3/4 cup coconut milk
4 ripe bananas, sliced (reserve one banana for garnish)
1/2 cup shredded, unsweetened coconut (divided use)

1. Bring soy milk and water to a boil and stir in dry ingredients. Add coconut milk and remove from heat. Mix well and cool slightly.
2. Fold in 3 bananas and 1/3 cup of coconut.
3. Pour into a serving bowl and attractively garnish the top with the remaining sliced banana. Sprinkle the remaining coconut over the top and chill until firm.

Insights: Coconut milk can be made fresh in a juicer or purchased in a can. To make it fresh, pierce two eyes of a coconut with a nail and drain the milky liquid into a glass. Crack the shell with a hammer and remove the firm flesh using a flat blade screwdriver. Peel the brown skin from the coconut meat with a potato peeler. After juicing, retain the pulp to use in cookies, candies, and cereals, or feed it to your canine companions. Coconut is high in saturated fats, so use it sparingly.

French Raspberry Parfait

serves 6

1 Tbsp. agar flakes (1 tsp. powdered), soaked in 1/2 cup
  water for 10 minutes
4–5 ounces soft silken tofu, puréed until
  smooth and creamy
2/3 cup raw unsalted cashews, soaked for 12 hours, rinsed
  and drained
2/3 cup water
2/3 cup brown rice syrup
1 tsp. vanilla
3–4 cups fresh or frozen raspberries
8–12 fresh mint leaves

1. Simmer agar in water for 15 minutes until dissolved.
   (Five minutes for powdered agar.)
2. Purée remaining ingredients, except for raspberries and mint,
   in blender, until completely smooth and creamy. Add dissolved agar and mix again.
3. Fold in raspberries, retaining a few to use as a decorative
   garnish.
4. Spoon parfaits into individual serving dishes and chill.
   Garnish with a few fresh raspberries and mint leaves prior
   to serving.

A feast for the eyes, this par-
fait is beautiful to look at
and delicately delicious!
It's an exquisite dessert you can
serve to your most discerning
guests.

*Guardian Angel,
please help me
feel the love of
Universal Life Force
flowing through me.*

We can thank our Latin American neighbors for introducing many delightful foods into our culture, including chocolate. This *Chocolate Orange Pudding* is a luscious celebration of Mexico!

Guardian Angel, please help me be in alignment with my true purpose.

Mexican Chocolate Orange Pudding

serves 8

2 Tbsp. agar-agar flakes (or 2 tsp. powder), soaked for 10 minutes in 1/2 cup water
1/4 cup concentrated orange juice
1/2 cup raw unsalted cashews
1/2 cup water
10 1/2 ounces (1 carton) silken tofu, drained and crumbled
3 T. unsweetened cocoa (or carob powder)
1 Tbsp. powdered grain beverage (coffee substitute)
1/2 tsp. orange extract
1/4 cup Sucanat® (dehydrated sugar cane juice)
1/2 cup brown rice syrup
1 Tbsp. vanilla extract
2 Tbsp. arrowroot in 2 Tbsp. water
5 tsp. powdered vegan egg replacer (Ener-G® brand)
6 Tbsp. water

1. Place agar and water in a saucepan for 15 minutes to soak. After soaking, bring it to a simmer, stirring frequently, for 5 minutes. Add concentrated orange juice and continue cooking for another 10 minutes, or until agar is dissolved.

2. While the agar and orange juice are simmering, place the cashews and 1/2 cup water in a blender and thoroughly liquefy.

3. Add the tofu, cocoa, grain beverage, orange extract, Sucanat®, rice syrup, and vanilla to the cashew milk in the blender and purée.

4. Put blended mixture in a heavy pot and bring it to a simmer, stirring constantly for about 5 minutes.

5. When the agar mixture has dissolved, add it to the pot and continue simmering another 5 minutes. (If the mixture is not completely smooth at this time, return it to the blender and purée; then add it back to the pot, returning it to a simmer.)

6. Add arrowroot-water mixture and cook for 45 seconds, stirring constantly. Remove from heat and allow to cool for 15 minutes.

7. When mixture has cooled slightly, combine egg substitute and water and beat to form soft peaks.

8. Fold the beaten egg substitute thoroughly into the pudding.

9. Pour mixture into an airtight container and chill for 2 to 3 hours.

10. Before serving, beat pudding with a hand mixer until fluffy.

Feel free to substitute carob for chocolate in this recipe, and it will still be sinfully rich and delicious!

Guardian Angel,
please support me
in creating Health,
Joy, and Abundance.

Reading, Retreats & Resources Guide

Suggested Readings:

Bernard, Neal, *The Power of Your Plate*
Cousins, Dr. Gabriel, *Conscious Eating*
Cousins, Dr. Gabriel, *The Seven Fold Peace*
Gerber, Dr. Richard, *Vibrational Medicine*
Hay, Louise L., *You Can Heal Your Life*
Howard, Jane M., *Commune with the Angels*
Jensen, Dr. Bernard, *Health Magic Through Chlorophyll*
Klaper, Dr. Michael, *Vegan Nutrition, Pure & Simple*
Kulvinskas, Viktoras, *Survival into the 21st Century*
Meyerowitz, Steve, *Wheatgrass, Natures Finest Medicine*
Pickarski, Ron, *Friendly Foods*
Raymond, Jennifer, *The Peaceful Palate*
Robbins, John, *Diet for a New America*
Szekely, Edmond, *Essene Gospel of Peace*
Thomkins, Peter and Bird, Christopher, *The Secret Life of Plants*
Wigmore, Dr. Ann, *The Sprouting Book*
Williamson, Marianne, *Illuminata*

Videos:

Catalogue available through the American Vegan Society, (609) 694-2887
Diet for a New America, with John Robbins
Forget Cooking; Prepare and Enjoy Living Foods! with Cherie Soria
Friendly Foods, with Ron Pickarski
Kitchen Gardening; Sprouting a New Leaf on Life, with Cherie Soria
Nutrition for Optimum Health, with Michael Klaper, M.D.
The Scientific Basis of Vegetarianism, with William Harris, M.D.

Retreats:

Ann Wigmore Foundation, 196 Commonwealth Ave, Boston, MA 02116 (617) 267-942
Ann Wigmore Foundation, PO Box 429, Rincon, Puerto Rico 00677 (809) 868-6307
Hippocrates Health Institute, 1443 Palmdale Court, W. Palm Beach, FL 33411 (800) 842-2125
International Essene Gathering, 45 N. Third St., Creswell, OR 97426 (541) 895-2190
Tree of Life Rejuvenation Center, PO Box 1080, Patagonia, AZ. 85624 (602) 394-2060
Optimum Health Institute, 6970 Central Ave, Lemon Grove, CA 82042 (619) 464-3346
Vegetarian Summerfest (held one week each summer), NAVS, (518) 568-7970

Resources for Books, Seeds, Sprouting Supplies and Equipment:

American Vegan Society (books), PO Box H, Malaga, NJ 08328-0908 (609) 694-2887
Ann Wigmore Foundation, (all) 196 Commonwealth Ave, Boston, MA 02116 (617) 267-942
Jaffe Bros. Inc. (seeds), PO Box 636, Valley Center, CA 92082 (619) 749-1133
North American Vegetarian Society, (books) PO Box 72, Dolgeville, NY 13329 (518) 568-7970
Optimum Health Institute, Seed Dept, PO Box 152808, San Diego, CA 92195 (619) 464-3346
Tree of Health (equipment), 3010 Gustafson Circle, Idaho Falls ID 83402-4639 (800) 944-5235

Organizations:

American Vegan Society, PO Box H, Malaga, NJ 08328-0908 (609) 694-2887
Biogenic Society, IBS Internacional, PO Box 849, Nelson, B.C., Canada V1L6A5
EarthSave International, 706 Frederick Street, Santa Cruz, CA 95062-2205 (408) 423-4069
Essene Church of Christ, 45 N. Third St., Creswell, Or. 97426 (541) 895-2190
North American Vegetarian Society, PO Box 72, Dolgeville, NY 13329 (518) 568-7970
The Essene Foundation, 2536 Collier, San Diego, CA 92116 (619) 2981809
The Nazirene Center for Universal Studies, 112 E. 11th St. Suite C, NY, NY 10003
Vegan Society, 7 Battle Road, St. Leonards On Sea, E. Sussex TN37 7AA - England
Vegetarian Resource Group, PO Box 1463, Baltimore MD 21203 (410) 366-8343
Vegetarian Union of North America, PO Box 9710, Wash. DC 20016

Index

photo by Lawson Knight

Kim Waters is a multifaceted artist, finding creative expression in painting, sculpture, mural design, furniture painting, book illustration, graphic design for book and CD covers— and music as well. Born in Chicago in 1952, she moved with her family to Washington, where she attended school. As a painter she is self-taught. The daughter of artists David and André Waters and sister of actress Kerry Waters (who also paints), she has been immersed in art since childhood, and her highly detailed paintings retain a sense of fantasy and wonder.

The paintings of Kim Waters are imbued with the magic of dreams and imagination. While the strongest influences on her work have been the artistic and spiritual traditions of India (particularly the poetry of Rabindranath Tagore and the teachings of A. C. Bhaktivedanta, Swami Prabhupada), she has also drawn inspiration from medieval and Renaissance paintings, the Pre-Raphaelites, Celtic art, and even the music of George Harrison.

Kim has written and/or illustrated children's books, including an alphabet book and *The Butter Thief* (Bhaktivedanta Book Trust, 1980), based on an ancient Indian tale. She also illustrated *Illuminations from the Bhagavad Gita* (Harper & Row, 1991). The spirituality and culture of India have inspired much of her work.

To contact Kim for art consignments please write: 1239 37th St NW, Washington DC 20007.

Cherie Soria was born in Santa Barbara, California. She became a vegetarian in her early twenties, after reading *Silent Spring*, by Rachel Carson, and has since become an internationally known vegetarian cooking instructor, lecturer, and food columnist. She is a popular speaker and presenter of food preparation classes at international vegetarian and vegan conferences and is captured in such videos as *"Forget Cooking; Prepare & Enjoy Living Foods!"* and *"Kitchen Gardening; Sprout a New Leaf on Life!"* produced by The American Vegan Society.

Cherie also coordinates delicious living foods banquets for large events such as the Annual Essene Gathering at Breitenbush, Oregon and the Annual Arkansas Women's Festival of Healing Arts in Hot Springs, Arkansas. She has taken the teachings of the late Dr. Ann Wigmore, whom she studied with in Puerto Rico, and created recipes that taste as good as they are good for you.

Ms. Soria is also a certified hypnotherapist, Essene minister, and metaphysical counselor. She facilitates seminars covering such subjects as *"Higher-Self Awareness,"* and *"Meeting Your Celestial Guardians."* and has assisted thousands of people in becoming aware of the effect food and attitude has on their physical, emotional, mental, and spiritual well-being.

What you'll find in *Angel Foods:*

⋆ Over 240 delicious, cooked and uncooked, meatless, dairy-free recipes from fruits to desserts!

⋆ Answers to questions such as, "Which oils and sweeteners are best?" and "What can I do to improve my families eating habits?"

⋆ Dozens of "insights" about food preparation and selection!

⋆ Valuable information about kitchen equipment, ingredients, and resources!

⋆ How-to sections on indoor gardening and creating delicious milk, cream, cheese and yogurt from nuts and seeds!

⋆ 200 beautiful, inspiring, angelic communions—one on every recipe page!

Please send me _____copies of *Angel Foods* @ $17.95 each: $_____
        (Bulk discounts: 5-9 books — take off 10%
                10 or more books — take off 20%)

Plus 7.75% sales tax (California residents only): $_____

Plus shipping & handling for one book
        ($2.00 for U.S. $3.00 for foreign): $_____

Plus shipping for each additional book
        ($1.00 for U.S. $1.50 for foreign): $_____

                I am enclosing a total of: $_____

Please inform me of upcoming cooking demonstrations,
or other seminars with Cherie Soria in my area.   Yes   No

Please print (This information is for your mailing label):

Name _____

Address _____

City, State, Zip _____

Mail To: **Heartstar,** 3911 Antone Rd., Santa Barbara, CA 93110